A Declaration
of Faith

✳   ✳   ✳   ✳   ✳

A Declaration of Faith

* * * * *

BY HERBERT AGAR

The Riverside Press Cambridge

HOUGHTON MIFFLIN COMPANY · BOSTON

1952

In memory of my son,

CAPTAIN WILLIAM SCOTT AGAR,

who was killed in action in Italy,

June 5, 1944

Acknowledgments

*   *   *

THE AUTHOR wishes to make grateful acknowledgment to the following:

Harcourt Brace & Company for a quotation from T. S. Eliot's poem "The Rock"; Harper & Brothers for a quotation from *Themes and Variations* by Aldous Huxley, published in 1950; The Macmillan Company for a quotation from *The Historical Evolution of Modern Nationalism* by Carlton Hayes, published in 1931; G. P. Putnam's Sons for a quotation from *The Greatness and Decline of Rome*, Volumes I and V, by Guglielmo Ferrero, published in 1907–9.

Preface

What you inherit from your fathers, truly possess it
so as to make it your very own.

GOETHE

THIS BOOK is one man's contribution toward possessing
our heritage, toward answering the question: What is
the faith of the West? History and literature are used as illus-
trations — not to "prove" the author's beliefs but to make
them more clear. And the book deals only with the West because that is our legacy. We can "make it our very own" or
we can live impoverished; but we cannot possess the heritage
of other peoples.

Asia today is gladly ridding herself of our rule. But for all
her new-found independence she remains poor, overpopu-
lated, hungry — and she has learned from us a trust in the
miracles of the machine which will prevent her from bearing
such trouble silently. Yet she cannot save herself. And the
Russians cannot save her out of their present surplus. We
alone could truly bring aid; but first we must grow strong in
faith, which would permit us to grow strong in unity.

Without faith and unity we shall suffer still more class hatreds, more wars of self-extermination, dwindling humanity and mounting fear. We shall soon lack the strength to help anybody, even ourselves. So we can say humbly that upon our efforts to possess our own souls may depend the well-being or the ruin of man. The West has the resources and the knowledge, if she can find the inner strength, to check the spreading decay.

This book is written from a Christian point of view. But it does not pretend that most Westerners are Christians; neither does it suggest that we should adopt Christianity as a mere convenience, because we need a faith. To disbelieve in God is a misfortune; but to insult Him is worse.

HERBERT AGAR

October, 1951
Beechwood, Petworth, Sussex

Contents

*   *   *

Introduction

✿   ✿   ✿   ✿   ✿

Introduction

✫ ✫ ✫ ✫ ✫

In 1793, when King George the Third of England proposed to the Emperor Chien Lung of China that the two nations should have diplomatic and commercial relations, Chien Lung replied:

> As to your entreaty to send one of your nationals to be accredited to my Celestial Court and to be in control of your country's trade with China, this request is contrary to all usage of my dynasty and cannot possibly be entertained. . . . Swaying the wide world, I have but one aim in view, namely, to maintain a perfect governance and to fulfill the duties of the State. . . . As your Ambassador can see for himself we possess all things. I set no value on objects strange or ingenious, and have no use for your country's manufactures.

The industrial revolution was already under way in England. "Objects strange or ingenious," the products of that small island, were about to flood the earth and to change the fate of mankind. In the realm of culture, Doctor Johnson and Edward Gibbon had long since perfected their elegant Augustan prose, and most Westerners had agreed to settle in their own favor the acrimonious argument (dear to scholars) as to whether their civilization surpassed that of Greece and Rome. It had not occurred to Europeans that there might be a third contender.

And it had not occurred to Chien Lung, as he presided over his two-thousand-year-old empire, that anyone could be so benighted as to compare the pale-faced barbarians to the serene and virtuous children of the Middle Kingdom. We smile today at the double misunderstanding. Yet may we not show a similar lack of imagination when we ourselves look Eastward?

On se voit d'un autre oeil qu'on ne voit son prochain. The tale of the British mission to Chien Lung reminds us irresistibly of La Fontaine, whose talkative beasts and birds and fishes mirror the follies of man. The tale might have been written to cap the poem in which he says that we see like lynxes when judging our neighbors, like moles when judging ourselves.

We have learned little from the great fabulist, whose store of wisdom we reserve for our children. And we have learned little from history. Today we are still as astonished as George the Third to discover that the Chinese find us distasteful. We reply to Asian criticisms as if we had not spent the last forty years making our politics and our religion alike look foolish, killing our Western neighbors on a scale which might have startled Tamburlaine.

In our struggle against the solemn creed of Marxism we seem to have lost our sense of proportion and thus our humility, without which we shall perish, for we have no claim to self-esteem. We, not the Marxists, are the authors of the grisly years of slaughter since 1912, when suddenly our tranquil-seeming world shuddered and flamed in the Balkans, reminding us that we still lived on a volcano and that we had been stupid to relax our fears because of a few quiet decades. Nevertheless, we are heirs to a great heritage, which it is our duty to serve, and which we shall serve the better if we sometimes remember how we must look in the eyes of a modern Chien Lung.

With such a purpose one may search the past for lessons, or fables, without pretending to do justice to the ancient dead. History may be as lacking in plot or pattern as H. A. L. Fisher thought, or it may be as repetitive and as full of useful lessons as Arnold Toynbee thinks. In either case, if we use it reverently it should lead us toward a knowledge of our predicament.

The reverent use of history implies two acts of self-denial. First, we must not see history solely as a recurrent conflict between bad men and good men, bad nations and good nations, bad classes and good classes. That way lies an easy self-indulgence, in which the "good" forces are identified with us, the "bad" with our opponents, whereas history should make clear that the evil in human nature belongs to all mankind. And so does the good — our enemies are always partly good. Second, we must not see history as a series of steppingstones toward the twentieth century. "The generations of the past are not to be dismissed as subordinate to the later ones ... mere preparations or trial shots for an authentic achievement that was still to come. ... Every generation is equidistant from eternity."

If we refrain from these misreadings, history can help us to clarify our troubles and to diminish our most deadly fault, which is self-satisfaction.

The dilemmas in which we forever entwine ourselves are deeply vexatious. Impulse tells us to blame them on bad luck, or on other men. Only the very wise or the humble can remember that if the world is out of joint we must all have played our part in the dislocation. Abraham Lincoln took that view of the American civil war; but the members of his cabinet did not. On the whole, democracies resemble the intolerant cabinet rather than the patient President, especially if they possess cheap means of mass communication. Neither the popular press, nor the radio, nor television, seems well adapted to reminding man that he is an unstable mixture of evil and good, and that the most presumptuous mistake he can make is to assume that because he has fought and won a just war he can build a just society.

Lincoln knew the disheartening truth; but he reached his knowledge through lonely meditation. Our citizens are not now encouraged to meditate. By every clamorous device they are encouraged to impatience with the troubles that sprout round us like mad weeds, however often we cut them away. They are encouraged to self-pity because the weeds refuse to die. They are encouraged to believe that all would be well — in a fresh new physicist's paradise, void of weeds and even of snakes — if it were not for the wicked enemy.

If our fables from history do nothing else, they should at least suggest that this is nonsense.

2

The opposite of self-satisfaction need not be self-distrust. We can see ourselves unboastfully, we can even see our avowed foes unindignantly, without thereby losing faith in our mission. Indeed, if we are to serve that mission we must cultivate realism and abstain from wrath. And as part of this task we must re-examine the catchwords of political warfare with which we lull ourselves and abuse our enemies. These words are worn leaf-thin, like very old spoons. When we try to eat with them they break. Capitalism, for example, or socialism, or communism, or even democracy: they must be revivified if we are to use them for self-education rather than self-praise. As Mr. Nehru says: "Slogans are apt to petrify man's thinking . . . every slogan, every word, almost, that is used by the socialist, the communist, the capitalist. People hardly think nowadays. They throw words at each other."

Not one of the words is fundamental to our civilization. They stand for political or economic theories by which at times we have tried to serve or to indict our great tradition. But what is the tradition? And do we still believe in it? If not, we had better close the argument, confident that the future belongs to men of stronger faith. But if we do believe in it we should surely try to find a definition. Even Marxism, revised by Lenin and Stalin, will triumph over a creed which cannot be described.

Sometimes we talk as if our cause were Christianity. But this needs explaining in a society where so many of the churches stand unused, in a "West" which includes not only millions of agnostics who are as indifferent to Christianity as to Buddhism, but also the fierce anticlericals of France, Spain, Mexico and Italy. If a third war came these somber enthusiasts might be our best defenders; but they would laugh, or curse, to hear they were fighting in the name of God. Yet they pay more honor to God then those who recommend the Christian faith merely because it is useful.

There can be no excuse for Christianity unless it is true. If false, no honorable man would preach it on the ground that it diminishes class warfare at home or international warfare abroad. Atheists and agnostics and anticlericals alike would agree that man's relation to eternity, however deplorable, is more dignified than that.

If we count out the cynics and the timid souls who profess a religion because it may make workers or foreigners more amenable, and if we count out the open disbelievers, are we not boasting to say that our cause is Christianity? Yesterday, perhaps it was. Tomorrow we may hope it will be. But today we should find a less ambitious ground for claiming that the West deserves to be saved. We may claim that without Christianity there would have been no West. But before going further in our pride let us remember that the Lord looks coldly on those who take his name in vain. Christianity if it means anything at all, must at least mean an other-worldly religion which sets its treasure in heaven, and which not only has faith in divine Providence but submits to it humbly. This does not seem an accurate description of Western man in the days of Belsen and the atomic bomb.

3

Less pretentiously, but with equal vagueness, we sometimes talk as if our cause were democracy. And what does that mean? Many Frenchmen, Englishmen, and Americans read into the word whatever they like best in their national life. To some it means economic, as well as social and political, equality. To others it means liberty, which has always clashed with equality. Furthermore, many Spaniards, Portuguese, and Latin Americans read into it not what they like best, but what they hate worst, in modern life. To them it means exploitation masquerading as free enterprise, corruption masquerading as free elections, or "the vile despotism of the majority." This may be unfair; yet we must admit that Spain, Portugal, and the Argentine show little enthusiasm for the New England town meeting. And even Brazil, Chile, Venezuela, and Paraguay do not practice democracy as the average Frenchman, Englishman, or American conceives it. Nevertheless, if our cause is Western civilization these countries are part of it.

From the days of Hannibal to the days of Stalin, in classical times and Christian, Spain and Portugal have been sharers in the great society from which we all descend. And today their child, Latin America, is more populous than the United States and larger than the United States and western Europe combined. If they are all to be excluded from the "West," the concept not only becomes silly geographically, and senseless historically, but it applies to a sadly diminished group of men.

If we turn from the present scene and consider the history of democracy, the picture is no less confusing. Athenian democracy (like that of frontier Texas) was based on slave labor. Roman democracy ruined its land, and then its soul, by levying human tribute on the known world. None of this seems consonant with St. John's gospel or the Gettysburg address. To be sure none of it proves, or even suggests, that if we could grasp what gives our Western world vitality we should find anything which conflicts with the democratic creed. It does suggest, however, that we should begin with concepts at once clearer and more universal.

Let us remember, on the other hand, that just as there would be no West without Christianity, so there would be no democracy without the West. One may seek it in vain through Asia and Africa and the island continents, unless the West has been the seed-bearer. Have we uncovered a family relationship or only a coincidence?

Is democracy merely one way of expressing in daily life our Western tradition? Or is it the natural flowering of that tradition whenever a community can rise above bare subsistence? How can we tell, until we find an unambiguous

statement of where we stand? Instead of soothing ourselves
with adjectives of ill-defined praise, we should examine our
troubled hearts.

We need a statement that unites the centuries as well as
the continents. If we dare to believe in our future, surely
we must summon the courage to believe in our past? A statement of faith must be a statement of continuity. This book
will argue that if such a statement ever becomes possible it
will include the following points: first, no government may
dictate on matters of conscience; second, there is a natural
law which guards this prohibition and which teaches that
there are many things we must not do to our neighbor (for
example, we must not degrade his moral freedom or dignity);
third, there is a natural piety which teaches that there are
many blasphemies we must not inflict upon our world (for
example, we must not ruin the irreparable soil to make quick
profits on crops); fourth, there is a sanction for these "musts."
They are not relative; they are not temporary; they are true.

The fourth point is the most troublesome for modern man.
What do we mean, today, by the word "true"? Justice
Oliver Wendell Holmes, at the end of the First World War,
gave a popular but dusty answer: "I used to say, when I was
young, that truth was the majority vote of that nation that
could lick all the others. . . . And I think that the statement
was correct in so far as it implied that our test of truth is a
reference to either a present or an imagined future majority
in favor of our view." In other words, truth is numbers because numbers are power. If you would know the truth of
a proposition you must ask, "Who says so?" If the propo-

sition might affect man's conduct you must also ask, "Who will enforce it?" Thus, if the United States and her allies had not been able to "lick all others" in 1945, the Nazi statements on race and on blood-purity would have been "true." "Responsibility is merged in numbers, and not a culprit is left for execution." Presumably this standard, learned from his predecessor on the Supreme Court bench, inspired Chief Justice Vinson to write in 1951: "Nothing is more certain in modern society than the principle that there are no absolutes."*

From the standpoint of an officer enforcing the law this Pontius Pilate attitude toward truth may suffice; but for our present inquiry we must find a less discouraging view. So we shall argue — knowing that we do not speak for millions of our fellow Westerners — that the natural law is true because it reflects the will of God. It would remain true even if most people did not agree. To be sure, a relative and secular truth can also be attached to it; but where, then, is the sanction? Not in Justice Holmes' "majority vote," which may be revised by any gust of passion.

In view of the strain of brutality which infects human nature, partially corrupting the noblest souls, can there be any sanction for good conduct if the will of God is excluded as

* The dictum was attacked in the magazine, *Christian Century*, which said that Mr. Vinson's statement "plays into the hands of those who deny the existence of the moral law and, in public affairs, make the interests of the state the supreme morality. . . . So long as it remains the basis on which judicial interpretation operates, it is a threat to the moral future of the nation." And in another magazine Felix Morley commented: "Our whole system of government is based on the assumption that there *are* certain absolute values, referred to in the Declaration of Independence as the Laws of Nature and of Nature's God."

unknowable or nonexistent? The notion that men will treat each other kindly, for no reason except that they are kind, does not commend itself in the century of Hitler and Stalin. We have been rigorously reminded that there is no downward limit to the degradation of man. The best of us, if we fall into the hands or the habits of beasts, may be transformed into beasts.

Yet the mention of God is disquieting to many of our neighbors. "Why," asks Professor Le Boutillier, "must we 'fly to the will of God' for explanation — in a political issue surely the refuge of ignorance? Why call the law of nature an expression of divine will, when it can be adequately explained as human will?" We shall try to answer this question later, when we have looked at the history of natural law. Here we merely affirm that the concept is a bond of western unity for the very reason that it may take either a transcendental or a mundane form. And those who prefer the latter should remember that Sir Frederick Pollock, in 1922, agreed with Christopher St. German (who wrote in 1520) that the natural law was essentially the common law of England — a sufficiently earthbound body of thought to soothe the most inveterate worldling. In fact Pollock, stirred by Holmes's famous attack on natural law, wrote to the American justice in December, 1918:

> If you mean to imply that no one can accept natural law
> (= natural justice = reason as understood in the Common
> Law) without maintaining it as a body of rules known to be
> absolutely true, I do not agree. . . . If you deny that any
> principles of conduct are common to and admitted by all

men who try to behave reasonably — well, I don't see how you can have any ethics or any ethical background for law.

Holmes replied with a sentence which might have been written by Jean-Paul Sartre: "As to Ethics I have called them a body of imperfect social generalizations expressed in terms of emotion." Fortunately, Holmes was too great a man to be bound by his own petulant asides. In a more serious mood he wrote: "The very considerations which judges rarely mention, and always with an apology, are the secret root from which the law draws all the juices of life. I mean, of course, considerations of what is expedient for the community concerned." Since the "community concerned," for Oliver Wendell Holmes, was the community we are discussing in this book — free men seeking their salvation according to their consciences — he was a strong though skeptical defender of the West. But like many of his contemporaries he thought society was best served on severely matter-of-fact terms. He became cranky at the mere thought of an eternal truth.*

Yet the articles of a Western faith which we suggested —

---

* Since Holmes cannot lightly be defined or dismissed, we quote some of his further observations on truth and on the law: "When I say that a thing is true, I mean that I cannot help believing it. I am stating an experience as to which there is no choice. But . . . I do not venture to assume that my inabilities in the way of thought are inabilities of the universe. I therefore define the truth as the system of my limitations, and leave absolute truth for those who are better equipped. With absolute truth I leave absolute ideals of conduct equally on one side. . . . It does not follow that without such absolute ideals we have nothing to do but sit still and let time run over us. As I wrote many years ago, the mode in which the inevitable comes to pass is through effort. Consciously or unconsciously we all strive to make the kind of a world that we like." ("Ideals and Doubts," *Illinois Law Review*, vol. x, 1915.)

freedom of conscience, natural law, natural piety and an absolute sanction — have had an impressively long life. The last three were commonplaces to the classical world from which our civilization sprang. As we shall see, they were variously interpreted even then. They have often been perverted to serve man's selfishness, and they have been used as an excuse for violence and other evils. But there has never been a time when many of our ancestors — Ancient, Medieval, or Modern — did not think them true. In their simplest, least pretentious form they lie at the roots of our tradition.

The Christian church has woven these and many other pre-Christian doctrines into its own wide picture of man's place on earth. And it has added the freedom of conscience — the area where government may not rule. Christians and anti-clericals, agnostics and atheists, we must all seek in that great synthesis for knowledge of what gave the West a soul. For we Westerners can only be the children of our own Graeco-Roman, Christian past. We may prefer to be something, or somebody, else; but the preference is vain. Even if we abandon our tradition, we shall not become Aztecs or Chinese or Egyptians. We shall merely become as nothing: self-barbarized barbarians.

4

Finally, if we search backward through time — not systematically, but groping for ideas and examples which strengthen our will and weaken our complacency — we shall at least escape briefly from the parochial wrangles as to whether Great Britain did right to nationalize coal, as to how France should change her electoral laws, as to why the United States should call her half-controlled economy "capitalism." On some days these heated problems seem trivial, almost boring, in the face of the awful question: Will the West survive, with or without coal mines, electoral laws, economic witch-words? The answer must be sought not in physical science, not in politics, but in the soul of man.

Dante, Carpaccio, Palladio, and Racine; or Montaigne, Rembrandt, Bach, and Goethe; or Shakespeare, Milton, Wren, and Jefferson — the names evoke the majesty of the West. Everyone will have his own lists, depending on his religion, on his travels, and on the art he is privileged to know best. But each of the lists which we may construct out of our opulent past will be a list of those who sought to fathom man's soul. Even Jefferson, the deist, the eighteenth-century dilettante, the subtle, worldly politician, designed many buildings of an enduring beauty after his master Palladio, and learned many languages so that he might enlarge his love of poetry. He became the prophet of a natural piety, and made politics serve his faith.

Can the spirit symbolized by these names survive the wreckage of our forty years' war? Or have we come to the end of our Western story? Science can find no reply. If it made us all rich tomorrow, with a four-hour working day and a four-day working week, and our last enemies drowned in their own blood, we should still perish if we refused to face the question: What is it, this faith in whose defense we seem ready to incinerate half the world? What is it? And do we by any chance believe in it?

If a positive answer could be found, if we could agree on our destiny and our duty, we could start uniting our great society — as some of our ancestors dreamed of doing in the eleventh century. We could stop behaving as if each small piece of that society, each parvenu, self-idolatrous state, was endowed with exclusive "interests" and "rights." We could begin to think of our neighbors as "us" instead of "them." We have seen that the prospect of abundant, cheap, atomic power does not make men more brotherly. Perhaps the prospect of a common cause might help.

Chapter One

✩   ✩   ✩   ✩   ✩

The Human Predicament

Chapter One

Neither must we fall into the illusion that the foe is
alone responsible . . . and that we are merely virtuous
defenders of a great cause, beset by scoundrels. There
must be a dimension of faith in which, whatever our
loyalties and however justified our defense of them,
we recognise the tragic character of the human
drama, including the particular drama of our own
day, and call upon the mercy of God to redeem us
not from the predicament of democracy but from
the human predicament.

REINHOLD NIEBUHR

IN TIMES of fear and strife, contemporary historians can
seldom rise above the concept of "virtuous defenders . . .
beset by scoundrels." Later, their naïve tale of good and
evil leads to a reaction as crass as itself — to cynicism and
"muckraking." The heroes of stage one are pictured as
wholly selfish and greedy. Yet life seldom fits either pattern.

Life is seldom simple, seldom good or bad. It is a heart-
breaking and inextricable mixture. The disastrous periods of
history occur, not because devils have been let loose on earth,
but because men and women are faced with predicaments
they do not understand and will not control. Thus they feel
abused and afraid, and take to killing one another. "War is
the anger of bewildered peoples in front of questions they
can't answer." *

---

* This need not be true of wars between nomadic barbarians and a
civilized people, wherein the questions to be answered are simple.

War is also the supreme expression of the evil that fights the good in man's soul. It is not true, the trite tag from Vauvenargues, that wars are declared by the wicked and fought by the virtuous. We all share the guilt. War is the very mirror of man's predicament. Although it wracks him he cannot avoid it. Although it obsesses him he cannot even understand it. As we have said, the best explanation that contemporary historians find for a war is commonly a simple tale of black and white. From that, they often pass to an even simpler tale of black and black. Finally, with the wisdom of hindsight, they come to a middle ground. They dismiss their casts of heros or of demons. They discover that the war was part misunderstanding, part heroism, part vice — in other words, a section of the human soul.

Histories of the American Revolution offer examples of these three stages. During the first, or heroic, period the colonists were pictured as driven by unbearable wrongs to resist tyranny. After beating the British (and the Hessian hirelings) they proved themselves political as well as military wizards, crowning their labors by inventing the best of constitutions. The result was prosperity, virtue, happiness.

Thus went the tale for many years; but in the end it bred reaction. The selfless leaders of revolution reappeared as New England smugglers, or debt-ridden Southern planters, or frontiersmen who cared only for cheap money. The generals became jealous conspirators, more anxious to steal credit from one another than to fight the British. The statesmen who contrived the sacred text at Philadelphia were transformed into class-conscious bankers, seizing their chance to oppress the poor. Instead of virtue, wealth and happiness, the new picture stressed slavery, squalor and the murder of the red Indians.

At last — but not accurately until the twentieth century — the facts began to sort themselves into a mixed tale of unmanageable situations, of impatient but well-meaning muddleheadedness, and of "the tragic character of the human drama." Most of the colonial leaders had wanted a form of dominion status which would leave them loyal to the Crown. The British government had wanted to collect taxes to help pay for the Seven Years' War. At first there was hardly a man on either side who planned to split the empire. But London was too far from Boston and Williamsburg. Communications were too slow. The brusqueness and combativeness of men proved too great.

In spite of the political maturity of the English-speaking world, no one was able to devise in one decade a Commonwealth of Nations. So the great schism came, for mixed reasons and with mixed results. Many men died because of the failure to solve an intricate, irritating problem. But we now see that there were no eternal rights or wrongs. The heroic and the cynical interpretations were both false. We are left in the familiar world of perplexed self-satisfied men and women stumbling from one half-defined puzzle to another, each confident that his own motives are respectworthy, each certain of the depravity of his foes.

Today we may have compassion for them all. After a

hundred and seventy-five years, when it is too late, we attain that "dimension of faith" which Reinhold Niebuhr asks of his contemporaries. Our minds are chastened by the tragedy.

Can we never hope to understand in time? If the past is a repeated tale of half-good men killing each other for half-good causes, must we always believe that the present is a pattern of black and white?

Doubtless we shall always believe that our own motives are pure. Yet we know that our grandchildren will find that they were mixed, and mixed in the usual proportions. Fewer dead men would line the banks of Styx, "waiting the back return of Charon's boat," if we could sometimes make that discovery a little sooner.

We need not thereby become saints. We need not love our enemies; we need only remember that they also feel cornered. Yet even this may be asking too much. If the historian has to wait decades before he can escape from self-righteousness or cynicism, how can we hope to be dispassionate in the midst of the storm? Only, perhaps, if we follow Niebuhr's advice and "call upon the mercy of God," praying for light.

There is precedent for such prayer. We are told that God appeared to Solomon in a dream and said: "Ask what I shall give thee." And Solomon answered, "I am but a little child. . . . Give therefore thy servant an understanding heart." And God said: "Because thou hast asked this thing, and hast not asked for . . . riches for thyself, nor hast asked the life of thine

enemies . . . behold . . . I have given thee a wise and an understanding heart."

Whoever can pray today might well copy Solomon. We
may be wearing out heaven's patience in our search for riches
and for the blood of our foes. We may be nearing the end
of the human drama if we never think to beg for wisdom.
For we live in a time of catastrophic history such as the Hebrew prophets knew. And we are making a mistake which
they shunned. We are assuming that the woes which sur-
round us, and the greater woes which threaten, are all to be
blamed on other people. But the Hebrew prophets saw
through their gathering darkness the judgment of God. In
addition to their imprecations against the enemy they found
time to ask: "What are the sins of Israel?"

Among the Hebrews' many gifts to man this is perhaps
the noblest. They alone, faced with pain, exile, the death of
their hopes, asked, "What have we done wrong?" — *we*, not
our enemies. Thus they became historians as well as prophets.
They saw that if they were the bearers of a special message,
of a purer truth than that known by their neighbors, and if
nevertheless they went down repeatedly to ruin, they themselves must have been partly to blame.

Wisely, however, they did not let their humility lead to
tolerance of oppressors, or to thoughts of nonresistance.
Angry men to this day search the Old Testament for un-
kind words to fling at their foes. "Howl ye, for the day of
the Lord is at hand," said Isaiah to Babylon. "Wild beasts
of the desert shall lie there; and their houses shall be full of

doleful creatures; and owls shall dwell there . . . and dragons in their pleasant palaces." Such language is human and comforting when applied to one's oppressors; yet every imprecation upon an enemy was matched by a cold warning to the people of Israel who failed to serve the truth that had been given them.

This is the reverse of our modern Western mood. We feel ourselves the defenders of a great cause (like the Jews of old), and (like the Jews) beset by scoundrels: but unlike the Jews we do not face calamity with the question, "What have *we* done wrong?"

2

Before asking where such a question might lead us, let us look at some other incidents where war is the mirror of man's predicament — war at its most hateful, its most barren, war in the name of all that is good, but productive at the time only of evil. Even such war may bring a small benefit for later ages if it teaches us pity for mankind, friends and foes alike — pity and terror, if we ask how in the hour of our trial we may hope to raise ourselves above such follies. Let us begin with the wars of religion.

When in the sixteenth century the Western Christian Church split, the line of demarcation ran raggedly through what was left of the Holy Roman Empire. If we would understand the horror which then came upon the Germanies we must recall the background of that empire.

Toward the end of the eighth century King Charles the Great of the Franks twice crossed the Alps to protect the papacy. On Christmas day in the year 800, as Charles knelt praying in St. Peter's, the Pope crowned him Emperor of the West — a title which had lapsed since 476.*

The Pope's gesture toward Charlemagne showed a pleasing gratitude; but it led to a quarrel between the nominal heads of Christendom (the Emperor who now spoke for the ancient Roman majesty, and the papacy which spoke for the law of God) which was to destroy the unity of Europe.

Charlemagne's vast dominion, including France, Italy, and the Germanies — a veritable ghost of ancient Rome — did not outlive its founder except as an ideal. But until 1250 the Empire's claims extended to the German lands and to all of Italy. After that date only the Germanies remained, and the empire soon became little more than the private possession of the House of Hapsburg. Yet it was one of the fairest possessions in Europe, and potentially one of the richest. When it was torn in two by the passions of the Reformation the temptation to restore unity by force was very great. And

* Effectively he was Emperor of the West; but he may have had larger ambitions. Lord Bryce writes: "In A.D. 800 the very memory of the separate Western Empire . . . had, so far as appears, been long since lost, and neither Leo nor Charles nor any one among their advisors dreamt of reviving it. They too, like their predecessors, held the Roman Empire to be one and indivisible, and proposed by the coronation of the Frankish king not to proclaim a severance of the East and West, but to reverse the act of Constantine. . . ." If Charlemagne aspired to the Eastern throne, this is a tribute to his imagination rather than to his power.

the temptation for princes to seize lands in the name of religion was even greater.

The first stage of the struggle ended with the Peace of Augsburg in 1555. Catholics and Lutherans were put on an equal footing; but each secular prince reserved the right to decide the form of religion in his own territory, and to exile those who would not accept the established church. This worldly and cynical doctrine was expressed in the famous phrase: *Cujus regio, ejus religio.* In other words, a man was free to dissent so long as he did it in silence or in exile — a statement which is strangely reminiscent of our own days.

The settlement of Augsburg contained the seeds of self-destruction, because if whole populations might have to change their religion whenever a new prince ascended a throne each struggle over dynastic succession must shake the Empire. Men who might have refrained from seizing power for its own insidious sake were now doubly tempted to seize it for the sake of their people's souls and for the prestige of the Faith. This is a strong enticement for frail man. The inevitable day when it proved too strong came in 1618, over the succession in Bohemia. Political rivalries, backed by religious hates and religious excuses, produced the terrible Thirty Years' War.

No historian has done justice to the horror of those years. During the last half of the war, all meaning in terms of faith had departed, though religion still heightened the passions and gave sanction to plunder and devastation. The population of the empire sank from about twenty millions to about nine.

Wallenstein (who was murdered in 1634) had perfected a form of wolf-army, whose soldiers had no homes, no commissariat, no allegiance except to their general, no future except the prolongation of war. When such men marched across a province, 60,000 strong, they did not leave behind them shelter for a rat. Yet because they were neither paid nor fed they were economical to maintain. By a Gresham's law of warfare the other armies began to plunder on the same scale.

During the final ten years the Germanies were a ruined battleground for French, Spanish, Austrian and Swedish troops. Whole villages died out. The debauched population could only live by trailing after the marauders, so by 1648 one imperial army of 30,000 combatants had 130,000 hangers-on — men, women, and children. The stillness of death settled over the land when the soldiers were elsewhere. Most of the provinces did not recover for a hundred and fifty years. But the troops — men and officers alike — had grown to enjoy the seemingly permanent war. Fighting and plundering and raping had become their only acceptable pleasures.*

By the time of the Peace of Westphalia, in 1648, the Austrian and Spanish effort to restore Catholicism in the Protestant North by imposing Catholic princes had finally failed. But the important result of the war, aside from the ruin of the Germanies, which may explain much of modern history, was the cynicism implanted in the European mind on the subject of religion.

* "It is no fantastic conjecture," writes H. A. L. Fisher, "that the Thirty Years' War put the civilization of Germany back by two hundred years."

The long agony did not teach men to stop murdering in the name of God: it merely taught many of them to stop believing in God. Having started with a cynical use of piety they ended with only the cynicism intact. Religion was seen by millions as a curse if taken seriously, but otherwise as a joke.

"In the lurid light of the Religious Wars," writes Professor Toynbee, "religion now appeared in the guise of a sinister and anti-social frenzy. . . . It was an attitude of mind which sterilized fanaticism at the cost of extinguishing faith."

Unhappily for modern man the fanaticism recovered more quickly than the faith. Today we face the most monstrous of anomalies: a materialism as intolerant and bloodthirsty as a God-maddened Muhammedan warrior. If, instead of matching it with an equivalent folly, we wish to offer an alternative, we shall have to outgrow the notion that faith is a little foolish. In other words, we shall have to outgrow one aspect of the eighteenth century, which was so wounded by the memories of the religious wars that it took refuge in a high-minded but worldly enlightenment. The genius with which Voltaire pictured Christianity as funny and Gibbon pictured it as barbarous has added to the wit of our Western tradition but not to the strength.

And we shall have to outgrow one aspect of the nineteenth century, which thought it had found the best of two worlds: a religion which no longer ruled man's life, but which at least abated his conduct, and a materialism which was not wholly material, but which at least left man free to multiply his inventions and to grow rich. The philosophy which went hand in hand with this compromise was a complacent belief in progress.

In 1912, for example, when Mr. W. Warde Fowler was writing about the despair which swept Rome at the death of Caesar, he added that this was "a despair hard to realize in our days, when settled and orderly government saves us from all serious anxiety about our lives and property." Nineteen-twelve was the year of the First Balkan War, the year of Italy's success against the Ottoman Empire, the year when Bulgaria proved the usefulness of airplanes in warfare. It was the last year of the pax Britannica, the first year of Europe's new agony. Yet one may doubt whether many readers were startled by Mr. Fowler's freedom from fear. People felt safe in this world and well insured against the next. It was not thought good taste to foretell new deadly wars. It was not thought polite to press the query whether man was on earth for a purpose. At the universities one was expected to make mild fun of the past and to believe mildly in the future.

Today, the nineteenth-century compromise between a pale religion and a partial materialism has been overthrown by men who offer an unleashed materialism and no religion at all. The West, however, is not yet overthrown. It may still win the contest for men's hearts. Nothing is lost except the nineteenth-century effort to combine material progress-worship with just sufficient piety — in case life should suddenly prove to have a meaning. We cannot compete with the Marxists on such soggy ground.

Nevertheless, though we may laugh at it we must respect the nineteenth century and be thankful that it brought long peace and many alleviations of life's burdens to millions of people. Perhaps we alone are to blame for accepting its benefits uncritically, and for carrying its optimism into an age when easy hopefulness has become a crime. By 1912, swamped in success and in self-praise, we had forgotten man's power for evil. We gambled on too cheerful a view of human nature — a view which none of La Fontaine's sober seventeenth-century beasts or birds would have entertained for a moment. When large-scale war returned in the service of a new idolatry, the wars of religion were surpassed in scope and equalled in ferocity. Before discussing how this could be, let us look for yet another warning, at another religious war, this time in the world of Eastern Christianity. The war carried both sides to ruin.

3

We have already mentioned that the brief "revival" of the Roman Empire in the West, under Charlemagne, led to a strife between the Emperors and the Popes which afflicted half the Middle Ages. The first crisis came toward the close of the eleventh century, when the Emperor defied the great Pope, Hildebrand, who had declared that no lay prince should interfere with the election or the investing of clerics.

The struggle between these two proud men led Henry IV

to his humiliation at Canossa, and led Hildebrand to his exile and death at Salerno. It helped to ruin Hildebrand's hopes for a Christian Commonwealth. But if the best was sacrificed to the strife between representatives of Caesar and of God, Hildebrand protected his church and his civilization from the worst. At the eleventh hour he saved the West from the fate which in his own lifetime overcame the Eastern Christian world.

At Constantinople in the eighth century the Roman Empire had been revived with a strength, a solidity, a capacity both for war and for administration, which the rambling, disunited domain of Charlemagne never knew. The Muhammedan menace to Christendon, which was met by Charles Martel at Tours in 732, pressed far more savagely against Eastern Christians, who lived on the border of the Muslim heartland. The Franks under Charles met the pagans at their most extended point, after they had conquered the whole of North Africa, and Spain, and the stark Pyrenees. Even the feeble Carolingian authority was sufficient to send the Muhammedans back into Spain. But nothing less than a reborn Empire (no mere ghost of ancient Rome) could suffice to keep them out of Anatolia.

Born in armor and christened in blood, the new Eastern Empire became a formidable power. And with the strength of Rome it inherited the greatest Roman failing: the inability to distinguish between the things that are Caesar's and the things that are God's. There had been no place in the old Roman scheme for an independent church. Even Constantine the Great had planned not to set Christianity free but to annex it to the state, since there seemed no way of destroying it. But the state was dying and the church was growing, so the plan miscarried for the time being.

Where Constantine the Great failed, in 334, Constantine V succeeded during the eighth century. The Orthodox Church was subjected by the reborn Eastern Empire. The Eastern Pope, the Patriarch at Constantinople, was diminished into a civil servant to the Emperor. And the results were as bad as many wise men predicted.

Since the church was now part of the state, no one could join the church without joining the state. No one could take the Patriarch as his Pope without taking the Emperor as his King. Among all the fierce border peoples conversion to Eastern Christianity now meant the loss of independence. Since the usual method of conversion was force, it followed that those who might easily have been persuaded by a Roman army to give up a vague paganism for an unaggressive Orthodoxy had thenceforth to be crushed into political submission as well. Seven centuries before the Western wars of religion, the truth of God was already confused at Constantinople with allegiance to a secular prince. The consequences became clear with the forcible conversion of the Bulgars in 865.

These brave barbarians did not mind being Christianized; in fact they soon became ardent in their faith. But they fought the Empire and themselves to the verge of the grave rather than accept a foreign political rule. In their desperate struggle against subjection they tried joining the Roman See; they tried setting up their own Patriarch in rivalry to Constantinople; but for the most part they tried fighting.

In the course of the consequent hundred years of war Constantinople called in the barbaric northern prince, Syvotoslav of Russia. The Mephistopheles of warfare had been evoked. Before long the two enemy emperors were huddled together, trying to save themselves from the new ally.

Eastern Bulgaria, the battleground, was ravaged like the Germanies in the Thirty Years' War. In 972 Constantinople temporarily beat back her false friend Russia, annexed the scorched earth of Eastern Bulgaria, and abolished the Bulgarian Patriarch and the Bulgarian throne — whereupon the surviving western Bulgars chose themselves a new dynasty, a new Patriarch, and started a new war that lasted forty-two years.

We have seen that during the Thirty Years' War in the Germanies all meaning and all religion had departed by the time of the murder of Wallenstein. In the hundred years' war between the Bulgars and the Eastern Empire, the same was true after the defeat of Russia. Men went on fighting, no longer to win but to annihilate, because they had lost the habit of doing anything else. The war could not end until victors and vanquished were alike ruined.

Prince Samuel led the West Bulgarians. Basil II, known as "the Bulgar-killer," led the Eastern Empire. On one occasion Basil took 14,000 Bulgarian prisoners. Ninety-nine out of every hundred he blinded, and from the hundredth he removed one eye. The one-eyed were then sent forth to lead bands of stumbling, sightless men back to their king. Samuel died at the obscene spectacle, but another five years had to pass before the bemused armies could stop fighting. "The Bulgarians were swept away from their settlements," writes Gibbon, "and circumscribed within a narrow province; the surviving chiefs bequeathed to their children the advice of patience and the duty of revenge."

The duty was fulfilled. Although Basil annexed Bulgaria to the Eastern Empire and again demoted the Bulgarian Patriarch, the ruined Bulgars survived, albeit precariously — whereas the Empire at Constantinople gradually expired. In less than sixty years from the end of this war Anatolia was occupied by the Turks — and they were never dislodged. The Anatolian peasants had borne the long burden of the senseless struggle to see who was to own the Patriarch. Gladly they submitted to the delayed Turkish conquest. Gladly they became Muslims. The prime purpose of the revived Eastern Empire was to protect Orthodox Christianity from the pagans. This purpose was defeated because Orthodox Christians spent a hundred years killing each other in the name of Christ.*

---

* Some historians, including the great H. A. L. Fisher, write as if the fall of the Byzantine empire was caused by the "calamity" that Basil the Bulgar-killer had weak successors. But the true calamity had occurred before Basil's death, when the Anatolian provinces of Asia Minor, whence the emperors at Constantinople drew their best soldiers and sailors, had been made mutinous by the unending war.

4

The self-induced decline of the Eastern Empire led directly to the Crusades. And these in turn led to a deepening of the hostility between Roman and Greek Christianity which has been a curse to Europe. The division between the "two Romes" — on the Tiber and on the Bosphorus — could surely have been repaired on doctrinal grounds. Neither the problem of priests' tonsures, nor that of whether the Holy Ghost proceeded from the Son as well as from the Father, need have split Christendom. But behind them lay the ancient contempt of the Roman for the Hellenized East, and the reciprocal contempt of the Greek for the barbarian West. When, therefore, the Eastern Emperor Alexius appealed to the Western Pope for aid against the Turks, Urban II saw an opportunity, not of helping the waning power of Constantinople, but of recapturing the Holy Places for Rome. This the First Crusade accomplished, in 1097; but nothing was done for the beleagured civilization at Byzantium.

Ninety years later the great Saladin, Sultan of Egypt, reconquered Jerusalem. The Second Crusade failed to stop him and the Third failed to oust him. With the Fourth Crusade we reach a sordid moment in Christian history. Under pressure from the merchants of Venice, who alone had profited largely from the first three Crusades, the fourth (in 1204) was diverted from the Holy Land to the conquest and pillage of Constantinople. For fifty years the Greek capital was in the hands of Latins. Co-operation against the infidel was thenceforth forever impossible. The Turks established themselves in Europe, conquered Greece, and in 1453 became the masters of Byzantium.

The "Second Rome" was lost because the Eastern Caesars failed to separate Emperor from Pope, and because Christian unity between East and West proved a less cogent motive than Venetian greed reinforced by the ancient Hellenic-Latin feud. An unforeseen result was that a "Third Rome" arose at Moscow, with the Patriarch once again a department of state. Eastern Christianity has never been allowed to serve God except on Caesar's terms.

This summary of vast events does not lead us as far from our own times as we might hope. For many centuries after the suicide of Byzantium the West was spared the sacred state, the state which is also a religion. In the sixteenth and seventeenth centuries this sinister ghost from the ancient world began to invade Europe. It was almost exorcised in the eighteenth century; but since the French Revolution it has again returned to plague us. Today, we can all see the likeness of the Divine Roman Emperor in Marshal Stalin. In case we should miss it, he allowed himself on his seventy-second birthday to be hailed as God by the Albanians. We can all see the kinship between the captive Popes of the "Second Rome" on the Bosphorus and of the "Third Rome" at Moscow. In case we should miss it, the Moscow Patriarch in 1950 issued in three languages a book called "The Russian Orthodox Church in the Fight for Peace." It refers to the United States as "the rabid fornicatress of resurrected Babylon." Even the prose style is Byzantine.

Can we all see with similar clarity how far we ourselves

have followed the same black path? The Russians did not invent the modern version of the sacred state; they perfected our Western handiwork. The Russians did not invent the total war; they merely prepare for a larger one than we have yet provided.

Since 1912, when the self-destruction of the West began (symbolically, in the old lands of the Bulgars), we, not the Russians, have contrived a masterpiece of slaughter. They may have done their best to keep step, but they lacked the equipment to kill on Hitler's scale. They still send their victims to exile rather than to ovens. Even the atomic bomb had to be handed them by the West. Ours is the leadership in the decline of civilization. We must examine our own minds, not our neighbors', to learn what has come into the world to make us feel that wars of annihilation may again be necessary.

Perhaps the question should be phrased, what has gone out of the world? Perhaps if we believed in our tradition we should feel less threatened, because we could not then be weakened from within. Nevertheless, there is also something new in our world which helps to make us fight our wars as stubbornly as if we were the Bulgars and the Byzantines. This is the marriage of democracy to the modern sacred state.

5

Shocked by the senseless slaughter of the Thirty Years' War, the eighteenth century invented a more courtly form of combat. Small professional armies fought professional battles. Whatever the results, the urbane pleasures of society were maintained.

There was no conscription in the eighteenth century. There were no wolf-armies, unpaid and unfed, whose sole means of livelihood was plunder. The political aims of war were limited. For the most part, the disciplined troops refrained from those atrocities which make reconciliation impossible. There was no thought of destroying, or of grievously incommoding, a beaten foe. "Unconditional surrender" would have seemed as savage a notion as Basil's plan for killing all Bulgars or Hitler's plan for killing all Jews.

The virtue of such temperate strife is shown by the visit to the United States of Francis Jeffrey in 1813. Jeffrey was a famous critic, the editor of the *Edinburgh Review*. He was almost as well known in America as in the British Isles. Britain and the United States were at war between 1812 and 1815. Jeffrey was in love with Charlotte Wilkes (a greatniece of John Wilkes) who was living with her father in the United States. Impatient of delay, Jeffrey took ship for America in the autumn of 1813, married Miss Wilkes, "and then made a tour to some large towns, conversing with President Madison and James Monroe, the secretary of state, and patriotically defending the English claims. . . ."

If we think what would have happened to a German who called on the American president or the secretary of state in 1943 and "patriotically defended his country's claims," we can see how far we have retreated from the concept of "limited" war.

Jeffrey's exploit, indeed, marked the end of a refreshing interlude in the story of human slaughter. Already in 1793 — twenty years before this happy honeymoon — universal conscription in France had warned the world what the new nationalism, wedded to democracy, would demand in the way of sacrifice. Explaining the law for the mobilization of "all Frenchmen for the defense of the nation" (23 August 1793) Barère de Vieuzac said: "Liberty has become the creditor of all citizens: some owe their work, some their money, some their counsel, some their arms; all owe the blood that runs in their veins." The first article of the new law proclaims:

> Henceforth, until the enemies have been driven from the soil of France, all Frenchmen are permanently on call for the service of the armies. The young will go to battle; married men will make arms and move supplies; women will make tents and clothes and will serve in the hospitals; children will turn rags into lint; old men will be carried into the public squares to raise the courage of the warriors, to preach hatred of kings and the unity of the Republic.

Arnold Toynbee comments:

> Thus, at one stroke of baleful magic, the French state is transformed from a public utility into a goddess. . . . This article (the first of the new law) so deeply thrilled the deputies that they begged the rapporteur to recite it twice over; and each time it was cheered to the echo by men who sincerely believed that they were liberating themselves from tyranny!

The distinction between the state as goddess and as public

utility will explain much of our modern tragedy. It is more commonly expressed as the distinction between a state and a mere government. A government is subject to constitutional restraints; a state is not. Restraints on government stem from the distinction between the things that are God's and the things that are Caesar's. In a free Christian society the state does not exist. There is the nation, which is both a physical area and a metaphysical center for loyalty and love. And there is the government, which is allowed certain powers and denied others. But there is no state, sovereign over soul and body. Neither freedom nor Christianity could make terms with such a state.

Patriotism, on the other hand, concerns only the nation, not the state. Good men have always loved their countries: the people, the customs, the hills and rivers or the lonely plains, the prayers and the church spires, the nursery rhymes and the poetry. And they have loved the symbols of their common affection for their common land: the crown, or the flag, or the great monuments which recall the woes and triumphs they have known together. Indeed, it is doubtful if a man would be capable of a larger loyalty if he did not love his country in this sense. But the state, the abstract state, is a loveless goddess. She cares nothing for church spires or nursery rhymes, and she does not admit brothers abroad. She herself is the end for which man was made, and she thrives on blood.

This notion of the absolute state was developed in classical times. It was revived after the Reformation, at the time of Charles V and Francis I. "The bitter conflict . . . precipitated by the Reformation as to whether the Church or the individual was the ultimate judge in matters of conscience and faith had opened the way for a third party, the secular state, to usurp the claims of both contestants." But the full danger was never clear until the *élan* of democracy gave strength to the pretensions of the renascent goddess.

Toward the end of the eighteenth century, at a moment when war seemed almost to have been tamed, when the new industrialism was on the verge of helping men to new amenities in their laborious lives, when the cult of liberty was undermining the absolute monarchs with their absolute sovereignty, when the notion of limited governments deriving their powers from consent rather than coercion had triumphed on both sides of the Atlantic, the old curse of the goddess state returned in a new form, by the back door. Popular emotion was to replace the king as the source of unlimited power. Instead of government as a public utility, plus the nation (in the light of whose past and present all her children could find fellowship), suddenly there came this worship of abstractions: "Liberty, the creditor of all citizens," or "the unity of the Republic," or "the exclusive national interest," all peremptory, blood-stirring, dangerously vague. In the name of these incantations no wrong could be admitted. The demented politicians who served them gave orders, exacting obedience or death. And the armies of Napoleon carried the new frenzy to the ends of Europe.

By the end of the nineteenth century, statesmen knew

there was no limit to what the people would put upon themselves if the appeal were in the name of national rights. The West, therefore, was compartmentalized, divided from itself more completely than ever in history. Each small part of the great society was treated as if it were the whole.

Nations, of course, have their legitimate and private interests which they have never lightly relinquished. But the sin of the new democratic nationalism was the fanatic ardor with which each nation came to feel that its interests were paramount, exclusive, beyond reproach or criticism. Henceforth, and increasingly in the twentieth century, French (or American, Dutch, Bolivian) interests came first, though the West stifled. Frenchmen (or Americans, Dutchmen, Bolivians) were protected from "outsiders" though the Western world, writhing in its homemade shirt of Nessus, clawed itself to death. Gone was the hope of a wide commonwealth, united in terms of the things that are God's and content to deal with the things that are Caesar's through unpretentious governments. Gone even was the worldly hope of the Enlightenment — that if men would not respect each other they might at least refrain, in the name of common sense, from making each other's lives needlessly hellish.

The harnessing of democratic enthusiasm to the new nationalism is one of the most grievous events of our time. The outburst of popular hope and strength, the decent demand for liberty and security and self-government, has not been perverted solely by Communists or National Socialists or Fascists. Throughout the West democracy married to nationalism has given strength and seeming virtue to the paranoic creed that in the name of the state man may have a duty to impose hunger, unemployment, overpopulation, despair, and finally war, upon the members of his own society.

Let us not delude ourselves that modern wars are terrible because of modern weapons. They are terrible because of the self-idolatry of the modern state. In the mood of fanaticism which that idolatry engenders we would kill our neighbors in sufficient quantities if we had to do it with spears. Prince Samuel of the Bulgars was so delicate as to die at the sight of his mangled, blinded army. Our world has stronger nerves, or it would have expired long since. What are 14,000 crippled men today?

Since wars of religion (or of a religious fury) have returned to blight us, and since the human tragedy now expresses itself in preparations for the largest of such wars, and since future historians will doubtless find as usual that there was much blame on both sides, can we do nothing to relax the tension? Perhaps it would help to look at the chief fault of our opponents — always a congenial task — and then ask whether we too could have such failings.

6

The complacency of other people is often surprising. The complacency of communists, being extreme, is the most surprising of all. To take a trivial example, the French communist paper, *L'Humanité*, described a triumph of Soviet science: the successful transplanting of the heart of one dog into another. The paper then added that such work was only possible in Russia, where scholars are "armed with the Marxist-Leninist theory, a guide to [scientific] experiment for which there is no substitute." *

When the subject is dogs, the reader may wonder idly whether the writer is sane and think no more about it. When the subject is God, the complacency becomes more serious. But there too the Marxist knowledge is final: God will linger palely on the edges of man's dream-life until the revolution is complete, at which point man's control over his destiny will become complete and God will disappear. "When . . . man not only proposes but also disposes," wrote Engels, "only then will the last extraneous force which is still reflected in religion vanish and with it will also vanish the religious reflection itself."

We said above that the ninetetenth century had gambled on too optimistic a view of human nature. In this the Marxist-Leninist is as typical as Herbert Spencer. Having discovered some useful economic theories, and uncovered some impostures, Marx and his followers swallowed the nineteenth-century complacency whole. They thought they had found the meaning (and in fact the end) of history. Life had long been a struggle between the righteous and the unrighteous. But the righteous had now found the "guide for which there is no substitute." They would therefore triumph, and there would be no more strife, no more history — only a classless, changeless, sinless world.

* ". . . armés de la théorie marxiste-léniniste, guide irremplaçable de l'expérimentation."

Yet "sinless" raises a question that Marxism can neither answer nor evade — and because of this failure it has been driven to substitute Terror for the Old Testament fervor of its youth. Are morals relative? Does sin exist? Does "wrong" mean anything except an act that is inconvenient to the Party?

Marx teaches that the clue to the past and to the present is class war; that capitalism can neither be reformed nor induced to drink the hemlock philosophically, but must be exterminated; that the victorious proletariat will thereafter have no class below it (or above it) to exploit, so that the state will gently, inevitably, fade into the benevolence of a classless world. "Only then," writes Lenin, "will men gradually become accustomed to the observation of the elementary rules of social life, known for centuries, repeated for thousands of years in all sermons."

What could be less alarming — if we skip the ugly days when the old order is being done to death? But do the communists mean it? Everyone knows the texts in which Marx and his disciples "prove" that morality derives from the means of production. Change the technology, they say, and you change the "eternal laws" of right and wrong. Why, then, do they assert "the elementary rules of social life?"

Communists, alas, believe halfheartedly in both these affirmations. When the Terror rages morality is suspended — whoever opposes the Party opposes "history" and has thus no right to liberty or happiness or life. But when a judge in New Jersey sends a spy to jail for lying, the West is accused of insolence — of ignoring the rules "known for centuries, repeated for thousands of years in all sermons."

This is not hypocrisy: our view of others is easily critical — *On se voit d'un autre oeil qu'on ne voit son prochain*. The lingering vague shadow of faith in an eternal law gives a communist permission to attack us if we trangress. And side by side in the same soul lives the new faith that a People's Democracy has a duty to kill everyone who disagrees.

Let us not feel sarcastic or superior. The whole world suffers when a cause that has uplifted millions of hearts is betrayed. The failure of communism — the failure to accept sin and virtue as absolute, unchanging — is only an exaggeration of the failure that still haunts the West. As we look backward from our gloomy present, communism and national socialism and fascism are clearly the natural brats of our own materialistic, optimistic selfishness. They are all the aberrations of Christian peoples.

Communism fell into the hands of ruffians because its hatred for the existing order triumphed over its love for social and economic justice. Therefore its guardian demon, who taught that Terror brings power and power determines morals, triumphed over its guardian angel, who taught that right and wrong are everlasting and that power must not be used to coerce the conscience. And where but in our own West did the guardian demon learn his materialism, his contempt for the rules which have been "repeated for thousands of years in all sermons"? If we had not fostered this contempt we might even have won Russia into our family.

"The communism of the East says that there is no God, that the earthly life of man is sufficient unto itself, and that happiness is to be measured by economic success, by the accumulation of worldly goods. Was the creed of Jeremy Bentham so very different?"

Bentham gave a philosophy for ruthless anarchic capitalism — which in turn gave Karl Marx, burrowing in the British Museum, his false views of human nature and of life. "Nature," wrote Bentham, "has placed mankind under the government of two sovereign motives: pain and pleasure. It is for them alone to point out what we ought to do." And how do these sovereign motives speak to us, drowning the small voice which "superstitious" men would call conscience? "Money," said Bentham, "is the instrument for measuring the quantity of pain or pleasure. Those who are not satisfied with the accuracy of this instrument must find out some other or bid adieu to politics and morals."

In the first flush of nineteenth-century capitalism, with its heady promises and temptations, many were glad to welcome this calm announcement that greed was the measure of responsibility. "Never in human history . . ." writes Leslie Paul, "was avarice so well equipped by theory." In Bentham's world of utilitarian liberalism there could be no absolute laws, no final truths. The government, to be sure, was expected to keep its hands off; but the new proletarian in his mournful new town did not find that his conscience was thereby liberated. He found that his body was enslaved. When he recovered from the horrors which had been committed upon him he was ready to hear that he belonged to a betrayed revengeful class — no longer to a community. And later, when the embittered West had begun its wars upon itself, the eco-

nomic materialism and class hatred of Marx was easily transformed into the biological materialism and race hatred of
Hitler.

"Man is a beast of prey," wrote the John the Baptist of
Nazism. "I shall say it again and again. All would-be moralists and social-ethics people who claim to be 'beyond all that'
are only beasts of prey with their teeth broken. . . . "

From the animal who is governed by pain and pleasure,
with money as the infallible guide toward happiness, to the
animal who is governed by class hate, with Terror as the first
resort of politics, to the animal who is governed by national-
racial loathings (Spengler's "beast of prey," Nietzsche's
"jubilant monsters," Hitler's "youth before which the world
will shrink back"), is not the road toward Hell unbroken?
Since the road started in the heart of our West, may we not
find pity and a fellow-feeling for all who have suffered under
the philosophies for beasts?

If Bentham and Marx and Hitler seem too gross an exaggeration of our Western failings, let us turn to some milder
(but still humbling) examples of what some of us have believed. Dazzled by the feats of science, men seriously
thought they were on the verge, not only of creating comfort and happiness for the human race, but of creating a
better human race for the comfort and happiness. "We have
now reached a stage," wrote Karl Mannheim in 1940, "where
we can imagine how to plan the best possible human types by
deliberately reorganizing the various groups of social factors.
We can go on to alter those inhibitions which are the legacies
of past societies. . . . We can foresee our goal which is the

planned guidance of people's lives on a sociological basis and with the aid of psychology." If this means anything, it means that we shall soon be God — so we need not worry about small errors like the slaughter of ten million civilians during five years in Europe.

In the non-communist world we may not often find this level of crudity. Yet even among those who know better the complacency is shocking. It stems always from the same optimism about human nature — from the failure to see that if man's freedom is real it must offer the choice of evil as well as of good. The more man learns or invents, the greater his power in both directions. An increased control over his environment is just as likely to produce ruin as to produce "the planned guidance of people's lives on a sociological basis." Or perhaps they are the same thing.

It is not only the physicist who threatens us with more knowledge than our virtue can support. Karl Mannheim was probably right when he said we could "reorganise" the human character; but he was wrong in thinking we should welcome such power. Recent trials in Russia, and in the contiguous countries, suggest that man has learned how to alter, and indeed displace, his victim's personality, with a result not unlike medieval "possession." Here is food for a larger fear than could be roused by any explosion, even that of the planet. Death's face must be kindly compared to the face of a man who has the means, and the will, to change his neighbor's soul. Yet Mr. Charles Morgan quotes a friend who did not draw back from this horror. "Any progress is open to abuse," the man said, "but you can't bar progress for that reason. If you do, you don't get any place." This was perhaps Eve's view in the Garden of Eden, warmly recommended by the snake.

When men wake to the fact that power, in the sense of practical knowledge, may be a deathtrap instead of a gate to heaven, they often move from complacency to despair. In the light of our religion the one vice is as wicked as the other. In fact the one is the reflection of the other.

Here we come close to the heart of our human predicament. However bravely we talk of progress or of the conquering machine, our world is scared. On both sides of the iron curtain we are frustrated and afraid. Most of us believe in nothing but the bad faith of our foes. Some of us have carried this a step further and believe also in the bad faith of our friends. Very few have kept the calm sense of a mission which gave strength to our fathers.

Thomas Hobbes described it long ago — this mounting obsessive fear that corrodes the minds of men who believe only in power. They can make no covenants with their neighbors, trust no promises, unless the police are present. "For he that performeth first, has no assurance the other will perform after; because the bonds of words are too weak to bridle men's ambition, avarice, anger and other passions, without the fear of some coercive power." We are reminded of two loud-mouthed men in a frontier bar, each armed, each eager to disarm, each scared of the other. "He which performeth first," wrote Hobbes, "does but betray himself to his enemy." Neither can in fact "perform" until the sheriffs arrive in force. But there are no sheriffs for our self-assertive, self-distrustful Leviathan states. They must calm their own passions by their own good sense, or they must fight. So we grow more scared each month. And the greater the fear the greater the boasting.

If, however, we could see the enemy's complacency, with its twin-brother despair, as but the mirror of our own, we might attain that dimension of faith in which we feel that we are all part of the same human drama, that we fight the same ghosts and fall into similar extravagances, that we shall be judged not by how hard we strive for the knowledge which is power but by how humbly we seek the meaning of our tragedy. Such an awareness might relax the tension, so that the loud-mouthed men in the barroom, seeing that they are brothers at least in folly and in the consequent pain of their predicament, might each feel less frightened of lowering his gun.

We seem a long way from such diminishing tension. On both sides we are still stiff with arrogance. We are still in the first, heroic stage of describing our struggle — the stage at which John Adams said of the American Revolution: "Britain has been filled with folly, and America with wisdom." That was a small war over a clear question — a question which could even be settled. Such wars rouse limited passions, and limited delusions of superiority. But the war that now impends is a war between pseudo-religions that we have not even defined. Religious wars create many times the problems they seek to solve, and continue long after the religion, if any, has evaporated. They are as senseless and as hard to stop as a Kentucky feud that has been multiplied by millions.

Not even the crusaders, in an age of faith, could keep religious wars from degenerating into cynical aggression.

Because of his own mixed nature man dare not throw away the sword; but he would do well to draw it humbly, knowing that the very deed is proof that he has once more failed in wisdom. If we must fight let us do so on the simplest grounds, like those of Charles Martel, who said "No Moors in France." And let us remember that we too will be to blame for the sorrows which will plague mankind. Let us remember that we had compartmentalized the West into selfish idolatrous states, lulled it to sleep with a religion of material progress, and begun the long horror of the repeated German wars, before communism became a force in the world.

Chapter Two

✩   ✩   ✩   ✩   ✩

"No Villain Need Be"

Chapter Two

In tragic life, God wot,
No villain need be! Passions spin the plot;
We are betrayed by what is false within.

☆   ☆   ☆   ☆   ☆

Oᴜʀ ᴘᴀʀᴇɴᴛ, the classical world, lost its freedom through war. The ancient liberties expired, "self-slain on their own strange altar." They did not die of barbarians, or of Christians, but of wars which the great society waged tirelessly against itself, wars which undermined its morals, wasted its land, dispossessed and alienated its poor, until there was no freedom left to defend. Since we seem inclined to follow a similar road we might profitably ask how, and why, our elders went about it. In the process we shall retell some of the best-known incidents in history. The reader may wonder why he is led down such well-beaten paths. The answer is in our daily headlines, which warn us against dismissing the problems of the ancients as old-fashioned or irrelevant. The more carefully we study them the more we shall find them unpleasantly up to date.

When we call ourselves the children of Greece and Rome

we mean above all else that we have inherited their concept of law. Alone among the great civilizations we and our forebears have tried to make law the unifying force in society — law, not irresponsible power, not generalized ethical principles of the Confucian type, not gnomic sayings or oracular anecdotes, but law with its precise definitions and its logic. This is the great divide between the West and the East.

The Socratic dialogues applied legal reasoning to the attempt to reach philosophic truth — something which no Egyptian, Chinese or Indian would contemplate. The science and technology in which we delight are the results of applying to nature the concept of the rule of law. And in politics the search for an abiding sanction for this rule has driven us again and again — Stoics, Christians and eighteenth-century skeptics alike — back to the concept of a "natural law," discernible in the heart and conscience of man. To us as to our ancestors liberty is a cherished word, but it means liberty under the law.

The Greeks failed to extend this concept beyond the city-state. Thus they perished of international lawlessness. The Romans of the Republic failed to extend the concept beyond Italy. Thus they were forced by fear into conquering Carthage, Macedon, and Syria, and so lost their freedom and their unity of spirit. Only in their tired age, and under a despotism, did the Romans show the ancient world what the rule of law might be. The West has never forgotten. And all of us who still live untroubled by a secret police should give thanks to Rome.

Yet the classical civilization failed at the point where we

too seem to be failing. After the Dark Ages, we of the West re-established the rule of law under the sanction of a universal church. When that sanction weakened in the sixteenth century the tyrant state came back to plague us. We escaped by restoring law in the form of limited, constitutional government, with the sanction of "the general will." Yet today, once again, the tyrannies are returning. When we destroy them on the field of battle they change their names and grow stronger. And one reason for this evil is clear.

Like the Greeks, and the Romans of the Republic, we see the fellow members of our own society as outsiders, potential foes, who must not share the benefits of "our" law. So we too have taken to self-annihilation. The free Greeks, when they had bled themselves sufficiently, were annexed by a despot. The free Romans were subjected by military tyrants. The free West has been undermining itself diligently since 1912. There is no need to blame other peoples for our plight. "No villain need be." Great civilizations die from within. We breed our own barbarians. The barbarians outside the Wall break through when those inside have done their work.

In this chapter we must give chief place to the failures of the classical world. Such emphasis may seem ungrateful, since we owe that world so much of what we cherish. But it was the fate of the ancients to be the inventors not only of our basic forms of beauty but of our basic social follies. We turn to them for the archetypes of poetry, history, philosophy, sculpture, building, and also for the archetypes of our political troubles including the repeated degradation of democracy into anarchy, then into tyranny, then into needless conscienceless war. Plato and Aristotle described the self-destruction of every type of government (except the theocratic tyrannies of Asia) in terms of what they had seen in their own small world.

Finally, lest the following account of the mistakes of others should make us feel superior, let us recall Mr. Winston Churchill's gloomy words on "the fruitlessness of experience and the confirmed unteachability of mankind." Our best chance to learn something from the calamities of our fathers will be if we can remember how seldom this has been done.

2

By the year 1000 B.C. the Aryan conquerors from the North, who were to become the Greeks, were established on the coast of Asia Minor, in the islands of the Aegean and at the foot of the Balkan peninsula. They had already lived their heroic age and were beginning to record it. The coastal farmers and seafarers had triumphed over the inland shepherds and were soon to found their first cities. Each city was to be built on a high place so that pirates could not surprise it; each was to become clearly, fiercely conscious of its separateness from the rest; and each in time would be faced with the problem of how to live on a barren land with a growing population. The solution in almost every case was colonial expansion. Thus the Greek colonist transformed the ancient world between 750 and 550 B.C.

By the latter date the shores of the Black Sea had been settled, and southern Italy and Sicily, and Marseilles and the east coast of Spain, and North Africa from Benghazi to Marsa Tobruk. The colonies were not private ventures for private gain. They were acts of state, under religious auspices, for the purpose of recreating the life of the mother city, who could not otherwise support her prolific sons and daughters. Yet even so the child could not share common citizenship with the parent.

By 550 further expansion had become dangerous. The Etruscans and the Carthaginians were contesting the western Mediterranean, and in the East the friendly Lydian King Croesus had been overthrown by Cyrus, the Persian. For the first time the Greeks were hemmed in: "Hellas was repressed from all sides," wrote Thucydides. Yet she could not stop breeding, and in spite of such drastic remedies as infanticide the pressure of population continued to mount. Under this pressure Athens remade her economy and founded her short-lived empire.

At the very moment when further colonizing became hazardous, Attica found that her sparse soil was well-nigh exhausted. Unable to feed herself by farming, she took to the sea and grew rich on foreign trade. The olive tree, that precious boon of the Mediterranean world, flourished on her bare land. And beneath her denuded hills she found silver. Athenian oil in Athenian jars, carried in a new Athenian merchant marine and protected by a new navy, gave her quick wealth and power. With her silver coins to expedite commerce she could now bring food and luxuries from the ends of the known world. Such was the physical base for the age of Pericles. The spiritual *élan* came from the triumph over the vast power of Persia.

Hardly had Athens established her new system when the Persian empire conquered the Greek cities of Asia Minor, pushed back the Scythian kingdom in south Russia, and began to invest Thrace. The next victim would be Macedonia, and then the whole of Greece could be subjected. There seemed small hope, since the tiny city-states of Hellas were as firmly separate as France and Spain today. They were forever warring on each other, and frequently rent with domestic feuds. They were also fertile in traitors: men who were glad to receive foreign money and foreign troops in order to put down their party foes at home.

In 499, however, the Greeks were given a respite. The Persian was called from his Thracian conquests by the revolt of Miletus and other Hellenic cities in Asia Minor. Athens and Eretria gave the rebels perfunctory help. No other Greek state moved a soldier or a ship. The future was all prefigured in this failure to unite, even when faced by a happy chance to make the Persians fight in Asia rather than in Greece. As a first result Miletus was razed to the ground. All the men were killed, and the women and children were sent into slavery. Then the Persian king, Darius, returned to his major purpose, conquered Thrace and Macedonia, and in 490 prepared to conquer Athens. If Attica had been seized and her ships destroyed, the subjection of all Greece would have been certain. Yet again no friendly neighbor state sent aid, or sent it in time. Only the near-miracle of Marathon postponed the punishment for such behavior.

The death of Darius and a revolt in Egypt delayed the next Persian attack for ten years and gave Athens time to build a still stronger fleet. Needless to say, when Xerxes finally invaded no two city-states could agree on a plan of defense. The chance for a successful stand at Thermopylae was thrown away. Athens was sacked and burned, though not until the population had been removed.

The last hope of Hellas was now her navy, which was mostly Athenian. Yet at the eleventh hour Sparta and Corinth nearly withdrew their ships because they did not approve of fighting in the narrow waters between Salamis and the mainland. After the battle, after this second seemingly impossible Greek victory, the Persian army withdrew to Thessaly, whence it returned in 479 to complete the destruction of Athens. The Spartans again did nothing, until the Athenians made plain that they were almost ready for submission. Then a strong Spartan army moved north, and with the help of militia from other states defeated the Persians at Plataea — this time more by the enemy's mistakes than by a miracle. At last, after a minor victory on the island of Samos, the Greeks were freed from the Persian threat.

This tiny, politically incompetent people had beaten off a great empire. In spite of Plataea the chief share of the glory belonged to Athens. There followed a surge of hope and energy which lifted the Athenians to one of man's great moments of creation. And Athens was rebuilt by Pericles, the fairest city in the world. But in politics there was no such flowering.

If Hellas was to grow rich and strong she must follow the Athenian example and turn to trade, to the overseas exchange of goods and services. This meant that the jealous city-states must become dependent on each other for their livelihood. The dependence would be intolerable, in fact dangerous, unless they could begin to grow together politically — to extend their law and their citizenship beyond the parish bounds. An effort was made in 478 B.C. when Athens and her allies created the Delian League. With her great fleet and her far-flung trade, Athens at once took charge of this maritime confederacy. She might have made it the beginning of true Greek unity. Instead, she quarreled needlessly with Aegina, with Corinth, with Boeotia, and with Sparta. And she turned the League into an Athenian empire, forcing her allies into the position of dependents who must pay tribute.

At the close of the Persian wars Athens had been the pride and envy of Hellas. Within thirty years she was widely hated. She had embittered the little world of city-states, poisoned its diplomacy, made possible the calamities that were about to follow. She had also contrived for herself a radical but impractical form of democratic government. The rash exaggeration of that democracy may have been a chief cause for the selfishness of the foreign policy. Step by step, as the stubborn cruelty of the policy unfolded it was applauded and pushed toward further excesses by the all-powerful popular assembly. No wonder Greek political philosophers of the succeeding age saw democracy as an accursed form of government.

The revolution that had made Athens rich had created new economic classes — men engaged in commerce, pottery, mining, seafaring. The new democracy was the result of these new classes, who demanded their share in government. Power shifted from a Council of Five Hundred to the popular assembly, which meant all the citizens.* The assembly had power to suspend magistrates and bring them to trial, so the executive did nothing but carry out the latest orders of the people. The Council now merely discussed the measures over which the assembly had final authority. A judicial assembly of 6000 members was chosen by lot. In groups of about 500 these "jurors" heard all cases. The verdict was given by a simple majority. The magistrates prepared the cases but took no part in the decisions.

This was indeed a pure democracy — at least for the citizens. Its failure explains the caution of the Fathers of the American Constitution, assembled in Philadelphia in 1787. It explains their attempt to insure for all time a division of powers between executive, legislative and judiciary, so that no branch of the government could dominate. Above all it explains their attempt to put the making of foreign policy out of the reach of the people. The Fathers gave such policy in charge of the President, who was to be chosen (they thought) by a board of wise, dispassionate Electors. And the President was to consult only with the Senate, which was to be chosen (they thought) by the state legislatures.

The lesson of classical history, according to many members of the Philadelphia Convention, was that the people (the electorate as a whole) is more inveterate in its hostilities, more ready to start large wars and less ready to stop them, than the

---

* At least 90 per cent of the residents of the Republic were slaves or foreigners or females, with no political powers.

privileged groups who have a wider knowledge of the world and of man's tragic past. The Athenian democracy had done its best to reinforce that lesson.*

3

Athens made her tyranny so odious to her newly-subjected allies that they were soon ready to turn toward Sparta, the city of militarism. Yet every Greek island or town contained groups to whom Athens still symbolized freedom for the citizen, whereas the oligarchic parties looked to conservative Sparta for support. As the self-destructive war approached, therefore, class bitterness was added to the other hatreds that were wracking Hellas. Revolutions and atrocities at home were the prelude to that larger atrocity which Greece was about to commit upon herself.

As Athens' trade with the western Mediterranean grew, so did her dog-in-the-manger selfishness. The rival cities felt that the greater her prosperity the greater their own peril. This was true; but it need not have been. Here was no "inevitable" or "natural" war. In that teeming and almost untapped world there was plenty to go round. But since the Greeks could not or would not co-operate they were compelled to fight. The Peloponnesian War began in 431 B.C. and lasted (with one brief truce) until 404: the Athenian

---

* Speaking to the New York state convention for the ratification of the Constitution, Alexander Hamilton said, "The ancient democracies, in which the people themselves deliberated, never possessed one feature of good government. Their very character was tyranny."

empire against a Spartan confederacy. Pericles died of a plague that broke out in Athens in 430, and thus the last statesmanly hand was removed. The brash Athenian democrats demanded "a war fought to the finish," which is precisely what they got.

In the course of the war Persia came back to bedevil the Greek world, this time on the side of Sparta. At Syracuse in 413 B.C. the Athenians lost the whole of a great army and a great fleet. Previously, on the island of Melos in 416, they had come close to losing their souls in what Thucydides described as the great central crime of the war. In a popular frenzy of hate and fear Athens forced the little Dorian Island to fight, besieged the ancient gracious town, killed all the men, and sold the women and children into slavery. She did not even take the women home as concubines, but handed them to any Thracian or Levantine ruffian who had the cash.

In the spring following the sack of Melos, while the Athenian fleet prepared for its own ruin in Sicily, Euripides produced *The Trojan Women*. This is perhaps the greatest poem of pity, the most moving lament over man's pointless cruelty.

> *The groves are empty and the sanctuaries*
> *Run red with blood,*

says the god Poseidon. And he warns:

> *How are ye blind,*
> *Ye treaders down of cities, ye that cast*
> *Temples to desolation, and lay waste*
> *Tombs, the untrodden sanctuaries where lie*
> *The ancient dead; yourselves so soon to die!*

When the war ended with Athens at the mercy of her enemies, Corinth wished to repeat the savage horrors of Melos. But Sparta, showing once more that the soldier may be less vindictive than the tradesman, merely disarmed the beaten city and leveled her walls. Athens was spared, said Sparta, because of her past services.

In the conduct of the fighting, however, in the treatment of the Athenian survivors by the Syracusans, or in the massacre of the Athenian prisoners-of-war after the final battle, there had been no pity. Atrocity ruled the day. Hellas seemed to have passed in fifty years from the heights to the depths, from Goethe to Hitler. In our modern world, not long ago, there were some who thought this a sign of our own superiority. Scholars even suggested that there was something "different" about the Greeks, for all their greatness, since they committed such crimes as Melos. But now we have seen round us the same crimes on a larger scale: the murder, the slavery, the revenge and counter-revenge. Thucydides now seems as modern as Mr. Churchill. The Melian tragedy might be enacted tomorrow in any of our pleasant fields or towns.

4

After the Peloponnesian War the political history of the Greek cities became repetitive. They never had a second chance to grow strong. The spirit diminished within them.

Instead of fighting new miraculous Marathons they succumbed pitifully to every conqueror. For sixty-six years they continued in a debased form their old fights among themselves — debased, because the soldier of fortune, the pure mercenary, came sordidly upon the scene. At the end of this interregnum Philip of Macedon conquered and united Greece. Then his fabulous son took revenge on Persia and carried Hellenic arms to the Indian border. After the death of Alexander in 323 B.C. and the partition of his empire into Egypt, Antioch, and Macedonia, the Macedonians kept Hellas in uneasy subjection pending the advent of Rome.

As proof that their political foolishness was unimpaired to the end, the Greek cities were waiting with innocent pleasure when the fateful legions arrived. They thought Rome would kill Macedonia, which was correct. And then, they madly dreamed, they themselves would be set free to resume their old practice of killing each other.

Hellas did not perceive that the whole scale of life in the Mediterranean world had been inflated. She moved blindly into the new age of much larger kingdoms, empires, cities, fortunes, temptations, and wars. Had she served loyally under Macedonia (whose kings protected her from the northern barbarians) she might have spared herself the final slavery to Rome. Had she formed a federation she might have contrived a balance of power in the Mediterranean, preserving the fruitful lively variety of her civilization from the monotonous Roman rule. But to the end the Greeks behaved like most Americans or Europeans when it is suggested that our own Western world must come together or die. The form of political association to which people are accustomed tends to seem part of the natural order. When a change comes, therefore, it comes too late, destructively, with wars and convulsions, insead of creatively with fresh forms, fresh thought.

Some scholars protest that we have no right to read these lessons into Greek history. They ask, "What do you want? The Greeks had genius but they did not have the compromising temperament that would help them to unity. How do you know they were wrong? They beat the Persians, built the Acropolis, wrote a large part of our world's best literature, and left us the priceless knowledge that liberty is most dear. Are you sure they would have done any of these things if they had cultivated the spirit of compromise?" Obviously there can be no final answer. Yet the more we learn of the diversity and flavor of Greek life the more pitiful ·it seems that so few of the city-states were given time to flower. They had scarcely solved the problem of feeding themselves when the Persians were upon them. Only forty-eight years intervened between Plataea and the Peloponnesian War. And after the fall of Athens the bloom was gone.

If we read Dr. Kathleen Freeman's sensitive and charming *Greek City-States*, where the life of nine so various and so enchanting cities is brought before us, how can we not wish that they had allowed themselves more time? How can we not compare them to our own Western world, also of great variety, great talent in the arts, great aptitude for self-slaughter?

Must the cycle of cruelty and revenge, atrocity and reprisal, always make nonsense of our love for beauty, grace, fair dealing? Can the good in our divided souls never provide a faith "stronger than anger, wiser than strategy"? The history of many lands and centuries faces us with the question, but nowhere more simply, more movingly, than in the brief tale of what the heaven-favored Greeks did to one another under that radiant Athenian sky.

> *When a still city lieth in the hold*
> *Of Desolation, all God's spirit there*
> *Is sick and turns from worship.*

5

Westward in the Mediterranean, meanwhile, the old cycle had once more begun. The scale was larger and the cast of characters more savage. The results inspired terror rather than pity.

As early as the year of Salamis, 480 B.C., the Carthaginians were warring upon the western Greeks. The Persians had perhaps urged Carthage forward, lest the colonies offer aid to their threatened parents. In any case, when Xerxes struck against eastern Hellas the Carthaginians invaded Sicily. They were soundly beaten. Their large army, fleeing inland, was captured almost to a man. The prisoners were chained and put on the land, where they won a strange revenge upon their masters: for as a result of this abundant unpaid labor a system of vast ranches developed in Sicily, plantations worked by gangs of slaves. In the end the slaves ruined the land. But in the beginning they ruined the free farmers, who were either bought out or forced out so that the big-scale, gold-mine method might spread.

Two centuries later, when the Romans captured these western Greek colonies, they found the slave-stocked ranch established. Although the whole strength of the Republic rested on the yeoman farmer, the temptation to copy the decadent Sicilian system was too great for Rome's youthful greed. In the language of Abraham Lincoln the new masters found snakes in their beds — plausible and alluring, like the snake in the world's first garden.

In 480 B.C., however, the Romans had but recently got rid of their Etruscan kings and were planning the conquest of Italy. The Samnites, the Latins, the gifted Etruscans, the ancient Hellenic cities of the south: step by step they were built into a compact empire, made loyal by a form of common citizenship, protected by fortified towns and military roads. What Rome took she kept — unlike the mercurial Greeks. The rule of law, not merely of the sword, spread across Italy. This was an advance on the Greek theory that the law, and the civil rights it conferred, could not extend beyond a city state. Yet Rome was soon to prove that she was still a long way from the vision of a law of peoples.

The very solidity of the new state made it intolerant of turbulent and less civilized neighbors, or of a strong established rival. The Gauls in the Po valley belonged to the former class. Carthage, the mistress of the Italian seas, belonged to the latter.

Failing some fresh political invention, some basis for international association other than master-and-slave, empire-and-province, Rome felt compelled in the name of security to go from conquest to conquest. The barren "Hobbesian fear" that we discussed in Chapter One was the chief reason for the wars which enriched and depraved the Republic. Not until her character was far gone in decay did she make war for mere capitalist gain. In her youth war was a substitute for political inventiveness. She could see no way of guarding herself except by the sword. Blindly fumbling for safety she degraded all her neighbors — and then found herself corrupted by the accumulated treasures of a thousand years.

There is no need to retell the history of that world-shaking slaughter. By 146 B.C. cisalpine Gaul, Spain, Sicily, North Africa, Greece,* Macedonia, were annexed. Syria was beaten but not yet made a province. The Republic stood alone, boastful but demoralized, amid the ruins of the society which gave her birth.

To grasp the full majesty of the destruction let us think of those iron years from the point of view of the Greeks. All round the rim of their Hellenic world, since the days of Alexander, new Great Powers had been building. With the rise of Rome the balance between them was upset; but no one dared imagine the rule of law beyond his own border. So because of fear, and the thirst for a lonely security, these Powers fought themselves to death on Hellenic soil. The Syrians were first defeated in European Greece and then butchered in Greek Asia Minor. The three Carthaginian wars were largely fought in the Greek colonies of Sicily and

---

* Greece was not strictly a Roman province, but was placed under the Roman governor of Macedonia.

southern Italy. The chief town of each district was laid in ruins. The four Macedonian wars were mostly fought in the Hellenic homeland. They led to the sack of scores of Greek cities. The last act was the murder of Corinth in 146 B.C.: the killing of all the men, the selling of all the women. Rome was "safe" at last. There was no one left important enough to kill, except her own citizens. This occupied her for the next hundred years.

We have seen that the Romans copied from the Sicilians the system of the slave plantation. The Republic was surfeited with slaves, since city after ancient city had been sacked. But the Italian land was limited. And the Italian rich were in a hurry to turn their abundant human booty into cash. The former Greek provinces in southern Italy were now public land. This land was quickly taken, within or without the law, by the same ruthless men who had presided over the ruin of a hundred kings. The soil was impiously ravished, and has not recovered in two thousand years. "Christ stopped at Eboli," the Italians will tell you today, if you travel through that desolate region where lately the fascist state farmed out its political prisoners.

Sicily and southern Italy, however, were not enough for the Roman capitalists. So the yeomen farmers, the pride of the Republic, were also dispossessed. Throughout the long wars they had been taken from their plows and sent to serve for decades at the ends of the earth. Now that the world was conquered they were returning home in inconvenient numbers. Many of them found that their farms had been sold or stolen — amalgamated into huge agricultural or pastoral factories which were starving the soil as well as the citizens, the future as well as the present. But the factories, during the first generations, could be expected to make their absentee landlords happy.

Cheap food and cheap debauchery, in the towns where the dispossessed were crowded, was the payment offered to the men who had conquered the world. Drunkenness and sex, both simple and perverse, usurped the old stern virtues. Private morals were soon as degraded as public. The desperate poor and the blasé rich shared the brotherhood of vice.*

This is the stuff from which class wars are made. "The wild animals that range over Italy have a hole," cried Tiberius Gracchus, "and each of them has its lair and nest; but the men who fight and die for Italy have no part or lot in anything but the air and the sunlight. . . . They are called the lords of the world, and they have not a single clod of earth to call their own." Gracchus wished to give farms to the disbanded soldiers; but the new rich, who had taken possession of the land, did not agree. So Tiberius Gracchus was murdered in 133 B.C. When the state has once acquiesced in a change of property rights, it is as difficult to change back as to revise a tariff downward.**

---

* "The nation was by this time simply a small and exclusive oligarchy of landlords and traders, bankers and concession hunters, artisans, adventurers and loafers; the metropolis was peopled with a noisy, unprincipled and self-opinionated mob, thirsting for pleasure and excitement, for easy profits and quick returns." (Guglielmo Ferrero, *The Greatness and Decline of Rome*, New York, G. P. Putnam's Sons, 1909, Vol. I, p. 57.)

** Later in the civil war, to be sure, both Sulla and Augustus gave land to their veterans. Yet in order to do so they evicted, not the rich with their cash-crops and their stock farms and their slave gangs, but the remaining yeomen who had survived previous depredations. Ironically, most of the soldiers who were thus restored to the soil had lived so long in frontier camps that they were no more suitable as farmers than as dressmakers.

The century that began with the murder of Gracchus, saw a revolt of Rome's Italian allies, wars with Jugurtha and with Mithridates, and three slave uprisings, in one of which an army of 70,000 maddened men ravaged central Italy for two years. It also saw the wars of Marius and Sulla upon each other, a Samnite uprising that nearly captured and destroyed the sacred city, the wars between Caesar and Pompey, and the wars between Caesar's heirs.

The conquest of Gaul belongs to a different and happier story. While Rome was ransacking the ancient world of the eastern Mediterranean, and losing her own liberties, she was bringing civilization to the West. The refinements of life, and a Latin coinage, and a wealth-producing foreign trade, were spreading through Gaul and across the English channel. Caesar went to Gaul, as Claudius went later to Britain, not merely as a conqueror, but to guard Roman interests and influence from barbarians or from anarchy. The towns of Britain and Gaul became self-governing communities under Roman protection. But this beneficent Rome, which saved the West for the old civilization, could not save herself from despotism.

The years of Roman self-destruction ended when Augustus won the battle of Actium in 31 B.C., annexed Egypt, and founded his weary but well-ordered Empire. By that time the army had become a long-service professional force. The ruin of the farmer and the bribing of the city mob with bread and circuses had become part of the accepted order. A sword had been driven into the body politic, inflicting a wound from which it could not recover. Rome was thenceforth two cities:

the City of the rich and the City of the poor. Statesmanship, which was at last to give that war-tortured world some intervals of peace, had failed to answer the problem of political unity until the hope of spiritual unity was dead.*

6

By the dawn of the Christian era the ancient world was content to be policed and protected behind the majestic Roman Wall.** It was glad of the golden autumnal sunlight after so stormy a season. It enjoyed the cosmopolitanism that flowered graciously within the Roman peace and the Roman law. Above all it enjoyed the prosperity that followed the peace and the law, and which, while it lasted, did more than all the legions to hold the Empire together.

Rome could unite the eastern and western Mediterranean because she had developed a body of law that applied between men of different nations, different provinces. This was her greatest achievement. It led her to seek legal principles common to all civilized peoples. It led her toward natural law, and toward the concept of a *jus gentium* that will forever give glory to her name.

* "The emperor's example at Rome was followed by the rich in the distant towns of Asia and Africa; they retained their grasp of municipal power by continually bribing the people with shows and food." (Ferrero, *The Greatness and Decline of Rome*, Vol. V, p. 348.)

**Physically, the Wall was not begun until the second century; but metaphorically it was there from the time of Augustus.

"A certain massive fairness and tolerant flexibility" were the mark of Roman law. A universal system of justice grew gradually during the centuries; yet like the common law of England it sought always to conform to what the "reasonable man" in a community thought right. The governors were urged to be careful of local traditions: "custom is the best interpreter of law."* And side by side with law went the imperial coinage, to facilitate world trade. During the two centuries between Augustus and Marcus Aurelius, save for a relapse under Nero, the gold and silver money of the Empire kept its value. And local currencies, like local laws, were not suppressed: they were encouraged to improve.

Men, money, and goods could move easily throughout those centuries, with light customs dues at Provincial boundaries, with passports unnecessary except in Egypt, with coins of an honorable weight. Yet the eastern half of the Empire was loud with clamor for home rule. Then as now, men of an old civilization preferred to conduct their own affairs inefficiently rather than to have "good government" thrust upon them. Egypt complained continually that Rome was no better than an absentee landlord, bleeding the economy. The fellahîn resorted to a primitive form of the sit-down strike. And the Jews rose desperately in 66 A.D., and again in 132, because Rome sought to obliterate their religion. (There was room in the Empire for Mithras and Isis, whose innumerable worshipers belonged to no centralized church, had no scruples about the official Roman rites. But the Jews were as bad as the Christians — clannish and well organized, dogmatic and intolerant of the state ceremonies.)

* Optima est legum interpres consuetudo.

In the Western provinces, however, there was no demand for independence. Rome had created their urban life and their prosperity; they were proud to be Roman. Rome meant civilization, and Latin was the language of the successful man. The West resembled the nations of the Commonwealth within the British Empire; Egypt resembled herself.

For all the majesty and wisdom of her law, however, Rome failed to impose rules upon her own rulers. By the time she had developed her *jus gentium* the Republic had been debauched and the government had become a despotism. There were no constitutional controls, no channels through which the popular will could operate. So far as the conduct of the emperors was concerned there was no sanction for Roman law.

And in spite of its revived wealth, the ancient world was tired. It had lost too much blood, condoned too many abominations. In its vigorous youth it had embraced inordinately the two evils which (as our West well knows) break the self-confidence of a society: foreign wars, class wars. The Greeks were so diligent in the first that they sometimes lacked energy for the second. The Romans, more robust, frequently fought both at the same time. When peace finally came it was the peace of exhaustion, not of justice and brotherhood and hope.

The failure of the first emperor in his dearest ambitions tells us how far the Roman Republic had undermined herself. Augustus tried to revive the old energy of the Senate to help him in his heavy task of rule; but he found the aristocracy degenerate. He tried to revive the sense of public duty among the people, if only to maintain a due proportion of citizens in the legions; but he found the democracy debauched. Desperately he resorted to stringent moral laws, decreeing, for example, exile and loss of property in the case of adultery — or death, if the *pater familias* should so decide. As a result he was forced to exile his own daughter, and years later his granddaughter, the former having been accused of nightly orgies, of prostitution in the forum, of taking a lover at the foot of the very rostrum where her father had proclaimed the new stern code.

No laws could revive the tradition of family discipline and public duty. No splendid imitation of heroic poetry, such as Virgil's, could restore the sense of religion as the base of Rome's greatness, or the sense of a sacred destiny which Rome must fulfill. Even the attempt to bring back the old military glories failed.

Among all the deeds of his imperial years the one nearest to Augustus' heart was the conquest of Germany. This was to give proof that Rome had recovered from her domestic wars and had remembered her civilizing mission — that she was not content to grow old quietly behind the Wall. With large expenditure of treasure and blood, Augustus pushed the frontier as far east as the Elbe, and at once began to introduce Roman laws and customs, and Roman taxation. Historians have suggested that if the line of the Elbe had been held there would have been no Dark Ages after the decline of Rome, since the Teutonic tribes would then have been as civilized as the Gauls. But in the year 9 A.D. the legions in Germany were trapped in the forests of Teutoburg. The commander committed suicide: the troops were butchered or enslaved.

Augustus had no recourse but to abandon all the country between the Elbe and the Rhine. He knew that neither a call for volunteers nor an attempt at conscription would repair the losses of Teutoburg. It was too late for the old youthful resilience, just as it was too late for piety, virtue, or duty. The future was a growing discord between the City of the rich and the City of the poor, a withering from within which the barbarians did not promote and the Christians could not prevent. When Rome fell she too, like the Greek cities after the Peloponnesian War, was "betrayed by what is false within." But meanwhile she had a last long evening to spend. And during that fortunate time Gaul and Spain became Romanized, and the Christian Church waxed quietly in the twilight.

In one great ambition, at least, Augustus had not failed. Two hundred years of peace, broken by a brief civil war, are his memorial. Except for local risings, as in Spain or Palestine or Britain, and except for frontier duties along the Wall, war had vanished from the Roman land, piracy from the Roman seas. When the bad times returned to the West the Wall had done its work and the barbarians were half-prepared for civilization. "At first I longed to destroy and beat down the Roman Empire," said Athaulf the Goth, "but . . . I chose instead to seek the glory of restoring completely the Roman name and of buttressing it by using the strength of the Goths, in the hope that later ages might know of me as the restorer of Rome."

The long peace and the rule of law may have come too late for Rome, when her stern civic and domestic virtue was already corrupted and her liberty lost; but they did not come too late for Europe. Rome had made the modern world possible.

"If a man were called to fix the period in the history of the world," wrote Gibbon, "during which the condition of the human race was most happy and prosperous, he would, without hesitation, name that which elapsed from the death of Domitian to the accession of Commodus (A.D. 96–180). The vast extent of the Roman Empire was governed by absolute power, under the guidance of virtue and wisdom. The armies were restrained by the firm but gentle hand of four successive emperors, whose characters and authority commanded involuntary respect. The forms of the civil administration were carefully preserved by Nerva, Trajan, Hadrian, and the Antonines, who delighted in the image of liberty, and were pleased with considering themselves as the accountable ministers of the laws. Such princes deserved the honour of restoring the republic, had the Romans of their days been capable of enjoying a rational freedom."

There is no need to quarrel with this famous description of the century which ended at the death of Marcus Aurelius in 180 A.D. Prosperity was indeed widespread, and perhaps even happiness of the restrained and urbane variety which Gibbon would have approved. Yet the "Meditations" of the last of these virtuous emperors suggest that the heart was growing cold within, and that Matthew Arnold was closer to the truth than Gibbon when he wrote:

> *In his cool hall, with haggard eyes,*
> *The Roman noble lay;*
> *He drove abroad, in furious guise,*
> *Along the Appian way.*

He made a feast, drank fierce and fast,
And crown'd his hair with flowers —
No easier nor no quicker pass'd
The impracticable hours.

The one plan that no longer occurred to the Roman noble, as a way of passing the hours, was to seek disinterested public service. After the death of Marcus Aurelius, therefore, when the line of enlightened despots came to an end, a new age of bloodshed and misery began. The army became the master of the Empire, raising or removing rulers by jealousy or caprice. During the fifty years after 235 A.D., twenty-six emperors came to the throne and only one died a natural death. The Augustan idea of the principate — the rule of the First Citizen, during an emergency, for the good of the commonwealth — was long dead. The Emperor was now "Lord and God." He was a military despot governing through a bureaucracy which was itself recruited from the army, and through a secret police which terrorized the citizens and abolished the last remnants of civil freedom. Now that citizenship no longer conferred liberty it was extended to the whole population of the Empire. Thus everyone became subject to military service, and could be charged a special tax in lieu of such service. And thus the gods of Rome, thought the Emperor Caracalla, would be placated by the homage of innumerable new worshipers.

Under this régime the economic progress, which had long been the cement of empire, withered. The falling birth rate, against which Augustus had passed his most stringent and useless laws, became a catastrophe. The old weariness, the longing for less bloodshed, which had made possible the founding of the Empire after the battle of Actium, now swept the world once more and made possible the reforms of Diocletian, which "gave order and system to the oppression and coercion by which the empire was governed in the third century," and "which simplified the whole machinery of taxation, adapting it to the primitive economic conditions of an impoverished and degenerate state. . . . Under Diocletian and after him the empire did indeed establish equality among most of its subjects, in the sense that all alike were beggars and slaves."

In the Western Empire, from the time of Diocletian, the long Roman twilight faded into darkness. Power was revived intermittently, and exercised erratically, for another two centuries; but the reason or excuse for power — the protection of a good life — had departed. Except for the plantation-owners in Gaul and Spain and Britain, the citizens were poor in worldly goods; and except for the small minority of Christians they were bankrupt in spiritual goods, increasingly sterile, exhausted in body and soul.

Even Gibbon, in his eulogy of the golden days under the Antonines, admits that the Romans were already incapable "of enjoying a rational freedom." People who have lost faith in themselves, and in the institutions which once gave them discipline, will revert to barbarism or despotism or both.

> "*Tyrannie must be,*
> *Though to the Tyrant thereby no excuse,*
> *Yet sometimes Nations will decline so low*
> *From vertue, which is reason, that no wrong,*
> *But Justice, and some fatal curse annext*
> *Deprives them of their outward libertie,*
> *Their inward lost.*"

The Archangel Michael was telling Adam and Eve about the troubles in store for their descendants. Enduring liberty will be impossible, he said, "since thy original lapse." But even a temporary, fugitive liberty must be founded on virtue, reason and reverence. When these high qualities decay, "Tyrannie must be." This is what John Adams meant when he wrote in 1787: "The people in America have now the best opportunity and the greatest trust in their hands that Providence ever committed to so small a number since the transgression of the first pair; if they betray their trust, their guilt will merit even greater punishment than other nations have suffered, and the indignation of heaven." *

7

Throughout our brief account of classical history we have selected and isolated the worst element in ancient life: the failure to find any grounds for union except force, and the consequent perpetual bloodletting. We have left out almost everything that made the ancients great, in order to stress their major fault. After Diocletian, however, there is little goodness or greatness to leave out — except the compilation under Justinian of the Roman Law.

In a later chapter we shall pass from the unfilial task of recalling the mistakes of our ancestors to the more pleasing

* This is also what Georges Bernanos meant when he wrote in 1937: "Non, ce n'est pas vous que nous craignons le plus, cher M. Hitler. Nous aurons raison de vous et des vôtres, si nous avons su garder notre âme!"

one of recalling how much we are in their debt. But here, before leaving the tale of disaster, let us remind ourselves once more that the great classical civilization lost its liberties in war. It could never collaborate with itself; it could only conquer and reconquer. To be sure, we have seen that Greece was united sixty-six years after the Peloponnesian war. But this was a barren and oppressive union imposed from without: the union of slaves and masters such as Hitler might have given to Europe.

And we have seen that Rome united Italy in the fresh youth of the Republic. Here was a new hope, a creative form of confederation which might have grown throughout the Graeco-Roman world. Yet Italy soon proved that she was as parochial toward her neighbors as the smallest Hellenic city. She had merely enlarged the scale of the destruction, because she had larger neighbors. It never occurred to her to enlarge the area of understanding.

Delenda est Carthago: Was there ever a more neat expression of the black madness which, when indulged, annuls man's virtue? Why should Carthage have been destroyed? A town of 700,000 people, disarmed after two defeats, shorn of her empire, but still busy, useful, cherishing the North African shore until it became the garden that Providence intended: Why should those men and women have been killed? Yet Cato, brandishing a basket of Carthaginian figs, enraged apparently by their mere harmless perfection, demanded that the entire city die. And so it came to pass.*

* H. H. Scullard (*Roman Politics, 220–150 B.C.*, Oxford, 1951, p. 350), suggests that the figs, which had been gathered in Carthage only three days before, were used "to illustrate the proximity of the danger." In any case, the fruit had an unsettling effect on Cato's mind and morals.

We can no more explain such wickedness on economic grounds than we can give reasons of self-protection for Nazi Germany's attack on Poland. Sovereign states, boasting their devotion to their own "enlightened" self-interest, may be seized by an insanity of fear or pride in which they mortally wound themselves. By the time Rome had no more "dangerous" neighbors, she also had no more soul.

At a certain moment in the decline of any people there comes what Arnold Toynbee calls "the irreparable event": the spiritual secession of the disinherited, the landless, the city poor, the men and women who have been too long ignored, who now feel themselves "in" the society but not "of" it. Thenceforth there are two Cities or two Nations. The City of the poor lives off the City of the rich, thinking itself a victim and being regarded from above as a parasite. The City of the poor has no loyalties to the society after "the irreparable event." It may lend itself to war lords, or bandits, or revolutionaries, for the pleasure of seeing the City of the rich destroyed. But its heart is elsewhere, perhaps sunk in apathy, perhaps preparing unconsciously to take on a new faith and to begin a new cycle. In either case the old faith is dead, and the society which it nourished is therefore dying.

The "irreparable" secession came to the Roman world after the self-disgrace of the Republic. The fabulous years of conquest, ending with the death of Carthage and Corinth, were intended to bring "security" to Rome. Instead, they brought luxury and ostentation for the rich, misery and dispossession for the poor, intemperance and a taste for reckless excitement throughout all classes. At some point during the civil conflicts which followed, the Republic simply expired in men's minds and souls. The City of the poor would thenceforth fight in anybody's army, for pay. It would accept free food and entertainments, without thanks. But it would no longer lead the disciplined life of the man who believes in his religion, in his country, in his children's future.

Might not our own West follow the same path? After the Second World War much of Europe came close to that fatal secession. If we would bring it back wholehearted we must attempt to make ourselves "safe" without drenching the Continent once again in blood. "L'Europe angoissée se demand s'il faudra subir elle-même de nouveau le cycle infernal: invasion — occupation — débarquement — libération." "Les frontières de la Russie sont jalonnées, comme la nôtre l'est de la mer aux Vosges, par les charniers des deux guerres. Les Français, les Allemands et les Russes ne peuvent plus se battre que sur des tombes, tant elles sont pressées."

If we cannot find "security" without fighting once more across those crowded graves, we too may wake to discover that our neighbors have seceded, that our own society has expired in many minds and souls.

8

The class hatreds which killed the Roman Republic and which led to what Lord Acton calls "an ill-disguised and odious despotism" were at the same time a prelude to the unborn

West; for in the disaffected City of the poor, throughout the Empire, Christianity took root. When the City of the rich had finally, methodically destroyed itself, the old world did not wholly disappear, because a new world had long been preparing to move into the vacant places. Of this the Caesars knew nothing: even those who thought themselves Christians belonged to the dead past. Their Christianity was a convenience of imperial politics. In their last agony they could think of nothing more original than to continue warring.

The oblivious Caesars fought on. They marched across frontiers, made treaties and broke them, decreed marriages and divorces and legitimizations, murdered their prisoners, betrayed their allies, deserted their dead and dying armies, boasted and despaired, fell on their swords or sued for mercy. All the tiny mechanism of power regularly revolved, like a watch still ticking on the wrist of a dead man.

Chapter Three

☆   ☆   ☆   ☆   ☆

"To Serve and To Keep Order"

Chapter Three

The choice of your way must be left to you, if the
authority that controls society is rational and friendly.
. . . It comes to serve and to keep order, not to
dominate where it has no moral roots.

SANTAYANA

IN THE ANCIENT WORLD politics and religion were inter-
twined. The sacred rites were performed by state officials.
Although a man might have eccentric private ceremonies
in his own house, he was not free to contravene the official
cult to which all citizens made public obeisance. The Christian doctrine that the state must not control the life of the
spirit was unthinkable to the orthodox Greek or Roman. The
Christians were therefore disquieting: they had moved into
a fourth dimension. They were hated for their seeming perversity. They were persecuted as antisocial nuisances. The
authorities did not care what the Christians professed in addition to the formal faith; but the whole pagan world agreed
that society was a unit, that obedience to the state must perish
if deference to the state religion were withdrawn.

The Roman Republic in its best days was a sagacious mixture of traditions, laws, and religious observances, each of

which strengthened the others. Faith was a support for self-discipline, designed to make the citizen a dutiful servant of the state. Property, family, happiness, life: these were negligible if Rome required them. "What the slave was in the hands of his master, the citizen was in the hands of the community. The most sacred obligations vanished before the public advantage. The passengers existed for the sake of the ship."

Although the old austerity had been corrupted before the dawn of the Christian era, the old view of religion remained. Since the Christians denied and derided this view, the state sought halfheartedly to exterminate them. Even when the persecutions had failed and Christianity had become the official creed, the emperors still thought in the ancient terms. The newly-promoted Christians were not intended to build a separate spiritual authority side by side with the government. On the contrary, they were to be absorbed by the government. Their church was to become part of the vast Roman bureaucracy, strengthening and serving the Empire.

This is what happened, as we have seen, at Constantinople. The old, rigid, all-inclusive and all-oppressive "state" survived precariously at Byzantium until ousted by the Turks in 1453. And it survives at Moscow today. But luckily the Western Roman Empire had become senile before it turned Christian. Neither the last sad emperors who still claimed sovereignty nor the barbarians who stepped across the Wall after it had half-fallen could prevent the Popes from preaching that no Caesar, however swollen his pretensions, should decide the duty of the citizen toward God.

The fame of Rome, sacred to the old world and to the new, was so great that the first wave of barbarians chose to preserve the city rather than to repeat the Carthaginian or Corinthian horror. Thus Rome was spared, and also the Pope with his growing bureaucracy. The Church alone maintained remnants of the dying imperial authority. The Church alone had knowledge of administration. Although subject in theory to the new northern rulers, the Church was the true power in most of the surviving towns. And in Rome she acquired full sovereign rights.

Long before the rise of new strong temporal powers, she had established the basic Christian dualism. Uncompromisingly she demanded control over the life of the spirit. She accepted and supported the mundane government, the political authority, as a useful agency "to serve and to keep order": a public utility, as we said in Chapter One.

Our own civilization, our Western world, was born when this distinction between God and Caesar was added to the classical concept of law. Religion, instead of preparing the citizen for subservience to the state, thenceforth protected him from the state so that he might seek his individual salvation. History was no longer a cycle of senseless recurrence. Life was no longer an empty pleasure or pain — dignified at best, hopeless always — but a Passion play in which each man must use his time on earth to fit himself for eternity. Hence the much-betrayed Western faith that no one, however humble, may be treated as a mere tool or slave. God has no second-class children.

The ancient world had caught the vision of a law which should be superior to nations: a law eternal, just, applicable to all. Until the birth of the Empire, however, it could not solve the problem of extending such law beyond parochial limits. World conquest was the prelude to the Roman rule of law. But the new Christian dualism offered a new solution: the universal Church, obeyed by all the peoples of the West, would give backing to a universal law. If temporal kings or emperors or barons ignored it, the Church would call them to account. No secular power, thereafter, would need to subject the nations of Christendom in the name of peace or safety. The law would provide for both. Within this moral unity the diversity of free peoples would flourish. Against this unity no external power could hope to prevail.

It was a sweet dream, and at moments it almost came true. The Church, freed from state control, seemed on the verge of solving the most inveterate problem of politics: *Quis custodiet custodes?* Who is to watch the watchmen, or rule the rulers?

We have seen that no Roman law could control the emperors. There was no sanction for their good conduct. Gibbon's five beneficent despots — Nerva, Trajan, Hadrian, and the two Antonines — might "delight in the image of liberty" and be "pleased with considering themselves the accountable ministers of the laws." But the last and best of them was succeeded by Commodus, who had other delights, and pleasures of a different kind. Who was to impose the law upon Commodus, who thought himself the incarnation of Hercules?

In the end his courtiers stooped to the most ancient of sanctions: they hired an athlete to strangle the son and heir of the great Marcus Aurelius.

We can scarcely say that the rule of law has been established when some good emperors follow it and some bad emperors are assassinated. The Romans could not answer their own question: *Quis custodiet custodes?* But the Popes in their pride believed that they themselves were the answer. The Church would watch the watchmen. And Heaven, presumably, would watch the Church. And justice would at last prevail.

The secular rulers might make such local regulations as they chose; they might devise forms of government as various as man's ambitions; but the Church would guard the Great Law, the law that was true and everlasting. And the foundation for that law was the Christian dualism.

Although the Church failed in her self-appointed mission, the West has never strayed far, or long, from the ideal of limited governments which may not coerce the soul. Indeed, the West would be impossible without the ideal. If this goes, all goes. And there are no grounds for compromise — although as usual in our mixed world there are times and cases where the rule may seem, through our blindness, to be inapplicable.

The Supreme Court of the United States, for example, decided in 1951 that eleven Communist leaders might be put in jail for preaching their creed. Such preaching at such a moment, thought the court, presented a clear and present danger to the nation. * The court may have been right or wrong about the danger; but unless we of the West use such powers sparingly, regretfully, and for as brief a time as is consistent with safety, we risk losing the soul of our civilization while defending the body. We risk a new cycle of religious wars if we revive the doctrine that the rulers may tell the citizens what to think. *Cujus regio, ejus religio:* we turned Central Europe into a desert the last time we submitted to that cynical phrase.

We need not accept the Christian idea of the soul in order to see the danger in this doctrine. The most worldly materialist will admit that each man has a private consciousness, a personality. If the government starts dictating to that consciousness, why should it stop short of a thorough, efficient remodeling? If today it can tell us what not to believe, on the ground of "clear and present danger", tomorrow it can teach us to take politely whatever the bureaucrats and "planners" have prepared. We have surrendered a defense against vast abominations when we allow the wielders of power to violate even one man's mind.

Yet politics are never logical. The best of the few choices

* The communists had been convicted under an Act which forbade conspiracy to teach and advocate the violent overthrow of the government. The Supreme Court, with two justices dissenting, declared that the Act was within the constitutional powers of the Congress. This decision makes a citizen liable to prosecution if he takes part in communist activities and if it can be proved that he had knowledge of communist aims. In 1943, on the other hand, with three justices dissenting, the Supreme Court held that an alien who was a member of the Communist Party when he became an American citizen could not be deprived of his citizenship because of that fact. The late Wendell Willkie represented the Russian-born Communist whose privileges were thus preserved.

that are offered may be most unpleasant. But let us at least remember that communism is not our only danger. We can also commit suicide. When we tamper with our time-honored principles, let us recall the warning of Jefferson: "confidence is everywhere the parent of despotism; free government is founded in jealousy and not in confidence; it is jealousy and not confidence which prescribes limited constitutions to bind down those whom we are obliged to trust with power."

And let us never be naïvely surprised that the state, if we grant it sovereignty over the mind, tends to turn its citizens into monsters. Millions of monsters, inflamed with an identical passion, are far more easy to manage than millions of plain men and women, each with private weaknesses and a private soul. The first aim of the tyrant, therefore, is to make his subjects as alike as possible. But when he has degraded them and robbed them of their inner lives, he finds that he must keep them docile with occasional orgies of cruelty.

Christianity, we have said, transforms man's life into a drama of individual redemption. No two such plays can be the same. But the despot craves an uncomplicated, uniform mob. The Church teaches that each lonely soul must seek salvation through the myriad decisions of its testing-time on earth. The despot seeks to diminish that soul to the animal level, where it will no longer care to decide. The Church seeks, therefore, to build an adamantine wall barring the secular sovereign from the realm of religion.

These crossed purposes explain the graceless treatment of Christianity at the hands of modern despots. And they explain why despots are driven in the end to feed their mobs on blood. The towering human passions cannot be simply dismissed, even by a tyrant state. They must still be used for good or evil. When the state finds that it can make no terms with religion, that God must join the long list of the proscribed, some wild new excitement must be offered to those who are thus bereaved of hope. Mass madness must replace the consolations of faith. So in one state we see grown men persuaded that they are serving "progress" by incinerating Jews. And in another we see children bowing to the same grisly goddess by denouncing their parents to a commissar and waving them off to Siberia. Even that world-conquering state which began by teaching the austere Roman virtues ended by debauching her citizens with spectacles of human sacrifice.

Unlimited sovereignty must always come to ruin. Physical power, which can easily drag man down, is unable to drag him up: the murder of Jews or of parents has a vicious charm when the all-highest Leader applauds; but no patronage, no Caesar, can make love more dear or less difficult.

Our knowledge of this hard truth, however often we betray it or seek to escape from it, gives the West its character and may save its soul. But it does not help our relations with the "Third Rome" at Moscow.

2

We have seen that the breaking of the last bonds between the Western and the Eastern churches, in 1054, was reinforced by the iniquity of the Fourth Crusade in 1204, and by the reciprocal contempt which the Roman and Hellenic worlds had long lavished upon one another.

Unfortunately, we have never found the sympathy and imagination which might have healed that wound. During the eighteenth and nineteenth centuries Russia — reluctantly but steadily — was moving toward the West. We did not welcome her politically or diplomatically, and as we grew farther from our Christian heritage, fell deeper into materialism, we lost the power of enticement. But we taught her the new gospel of Karl Marx. Today, therefore, Russia and the West once more confront each other with the incomprehension of a Greek scholar and a Roman business man in the days of Plutarch, of a bureaucrat at Constantinople and a Frankish baron in the days of Charlemagne.

No matter on which slope of the great divide our sympathies may lie in any century or any millenium, the divide remains. The boundary (which we recently, tragically, failed to abolish) has scarcely varied to the east or west in twenty-five hundred years; it has merely prolonged itself northward. In the days of Italy versus Hellas or Rome versus Byzantium, it was the line from Tobruk to Trieste. Now (with a few bulges) it is the line from Trieste to Danzig.

The balance of virtue, wisdom, genius has shifted from side to side of the line, from age to age; but the misunderstanding has been almost continuous. We take today's problems of adjustment too lightly when we ascribe them to Marx. Communism is a modern refuge for disillusioned Christians; but the tension between Western and Eastern Europe began when the Roman legions first met the talkative, artistic Greeks. The old suspicions and the mutual disdain were merely deepened when the Western Church took over the city of Rome while the Eastern Church bowed to Constantinople.

Yet we can find in our daily newspapers the proof of what might have been accomplished by high-mindedness. Because the West has at last begun co-operating for defense Greece and Turkey are now allied to us from the other side of the line. If we became a true society, loyally members of one another, much of the world would be glad to draw closer. There can be nothing exclusive about an association which derives from Christianity; but we can scarcely tempt mankind to join us until we have the good will to join ourselves. And the first step is to define "ourselves."

As part of the ancient and lamentable feud, Russian historians have argued long and persuasively that their country (in spite of today's passing madness) is the favored child of the classical world, the chief heir to the glory that was Greece. The West, they say, offers an inferior version of the true tradition, which was carried from Constantinople to Holy Russia.

An eminent exile has recently attacked Arnold Toynbee on this point. When listing the Great Societies of today Mr. Toynbee makes the Orthodox Christian world a separate civilization, like the Western, Islamic, Hindu, and Far Eastern. But Professor Wladimir Weidlé resents this wide division between the two offspring of the Classical-Hebrew marriage. The true distinction, he says, can be summed up simply: "Grèce fort peu romanisée d'une part, Grèce à travers Rome de l'autre." The result, he argues, has not been two civilizations, two Christianities, two Europes. Europe was born three thousand years ago on the eastern shores of the Mediterranean. Russia is integral to that Europe, and reflects it in a purer form than does the Romanized West. The differences between Russia and the West therefore are family differences, on a par with those between England and Italy, France and Germany. They should not be compared to the differences between one civilization and another, such as the Muhammedan and the Hindu.

In a most illuminating fashion this argument states the problem and misses the point. The West was not born in 1000 B.C. when the Greeks first came to Asia Minor and the Aegean. It was born when the Christian dualism was wedded to the Roman law. In Russia there has been no such wedding — but the fault may be largely ours, for in the nineteenth century Russia was drawing close to the West.

"Dieu, que notre Russie est triste!" said Pushkin. Generations of Russian novelists and historians have described those spiritually gifted people, melancholy as their infinite silent plains, indifferent to the mad tyrants who have seized power at Kiev or Novgorod or St. Petersburg or Moscow, seeking some private relation to eternity, some God or anti-God who might assuage the pain within them. Dostoyevsky's fellow countrymen have no bent toward materialism; but they have suffered for centuries under a church that belongs to the state and a state that therefore belongs to the latest despot who has usurped it. No wonder they find Russia *triste*. No wonder they give their hearts to the land itself, to the mystical Mother Russia, and seek to ignore politics. No wonder the bureaucrats and centralizers have always scourged them.

In our Western sense Russia has never known politics. She has kept intact the system of the Roman Empire: tyranny tempered by assassination. Without dualism there can be no rule of law. This alone would justify Arnold Toynbee in his distinction between the heirs of Rome and of Constantinople. But let us not think that it justifies the West in feeling superior. The more highly we prize our tradition, the more humble we should become at the memory of what we have done to it, and of our failure to convert the Russians.

We must turn now to our partial successes and repeated mistakes in seeking to make the Western dualism prevail.

3

The founder of the medieval Papacy was Gregory the Great, who died in 604. He could almost be named the savior of the West, which might have perished in infancy had he not broken with the classical past by deserting the imperial service to become a monk. The church which gave the West a soul, and the city which gave it a local habitation from which to spread, might both have perished in the sixth century without Gregory.

In 573, when he was civil governor of Rome, the capital of the Empire had long since been moved to the Bosphorus;

the Lombards had recently conquered northern Italy and were raging through the center and the south; the lands round the city, under effective Roman rule, were no larger than the fields owned by the little village which had set out to unite Italy a thousand years before, when Athens had but recently beaten the Persians and Sicily had just enslaved a Carthaginian army. But Gregory's Rome was not a self-contained village. It was the sprawling remains of a world-city, deprived of its provinces and its tribute, half-starved, and in danger of being put to the sword by a barbarian war band.

A rich man, with a conventional education, Gregory had labored for his ailing metropolis with that patrician sense of public duty which might have led an ex-courtier of Franz Josef to administer a precinct of Vienna in 1920. Suddenly, Gregory turned his back on the Rome of his fathers, resigned from the civil government, gave his property to the poor or to Benedictine monasteries, and entered one of his own endowed houses as a simple monk. * In a few years he was recalled by the Pope, taken from the life of contemplation to serve his immemorial city in its new embodiment as the Christian capital. And in 590, much against his will, in the midst of war and starvation, he was himself made Pope.

He sought help from Constantinople against the Lombards. But Rome had become a peripheral nuisance to the eastern capital, which therefore sent no aid. So Gregory made the

* St. Benedict had established the parent house of his order at Monte Cassino before 540 A.D. Thence his followers were spreading throughout Italy, reviving Christian discipline, and also reviving some of the Italian land for the first time since it had been ruined by the slave-ranches against which Tiberius Gracchus preached.

best truce possible with the barbarians. He saved the temporal power of the Papacy in the holy city, established the Papal claims to spiritual sovereignty throughout a West which was thus made conscious of its existence, and by a miracle of administration reorganized the scattered estates of the church, in Italy and overseas, so that the Roman poor were kept from famine. He gave such strong support to the monasticism of St. Benedict that it survived the wreckage of the following centuries. And in 596, when the Lombards were again besieging his city, he sent St. Augustine to far-off Britain, long abandoned by the Legions, to begin the seemingly hopeless work of reuniting the once-Roman West in the faith of the new Rome.

Gregory appears never to have thought that he was founding a society. He merely did all that a man might do to save the unhappy members of the society in which he lived. He did it reluctantly, out of duty, with his eyes on another world for which he had planned to prepare himself in silence and retirement. Perhaps this is why he built better than he knew. During his fourteen years as Pontiff he established in many hearts the majesty of the Papal city and the notion of a religion whose rule reached across shifting secular frontiers. And the monastic protection for learning and for the land was made safe. *

The Dark Ages had not ended; but the Middle Ages had

---

* The site at Monte Cassino had been chosen by St. Benedict with a view to defense against barbarians. Yet even before Gregory became Pope the Lombards had taken it briefly. It was destroyed in the ninth century by the Saracens, and twice again before the complete devastation of 1944. But the Benedictines were never finally ousted, and the rebuilding of the monastery goes forward today.

become possible. Western Christendon had survived its perilous beginnings. Four centuries later another Pope, who took the name of Gregory VII, was to come close to building that commonwealth of the spirit which Gregory the Great had foreshadowed. But first came the prodigious Emperor Charles.

4

We mentioned in Chapter One that on Christmas Day in the year 800 Pope Leo III named Charlemagne Emperor of the West, thus preparing the way for war between the revived Empire and the Vatican. The Vicar of Christ might claim a large authority over mere kings; but who was to give orders to the successor of Augustus Caesar? Later, when Popes and Emperors had grown stronger and more ambitious, the question became desperate; but at first all went smoothly between the two "supreme" powers.

A previous Pope had given his blessing when the father of Charlemagne seized the Frankish crown — and he had accepted as reward the dubious gift of the Papal States. For eleven hundred years central Italy was to remain politically subject to the Church. Ill-governed and disorderly, the unhappy land was a standing invitation to plunder. The first of many powers to accept the invitation was the Lombard king whom Charles, at the request of the Pope, defeated in

773. The crown of Lombardy then passed to the Frankish rulers; the Papal States were restored to Rome.

Twenty-six years later, in 799, the ever rebellious Romans rose against Leo III, who fled to the court of Charles and asked to be reinstated. But his subjects had accused him, among other improprieties, of adultery and the sale of sacred offices. Charles was a man of simple piety who had no wish to restore a bad Pope or to betray a good one. Yet where in all Christendom was there an authority fit to pass on such a case?

The Eastern and Western Churches had briefly composed their quarrels and were for the time united; but no Frankish king could accept the servile Patriarch as judge over his own Pope. The Eastern Emperor still thought himself the lord of the whole Christian world; but for centuries the West had denied his claims. And in any case the Eastern Emperor was a woman in 799 — and a most unsuitable woman, who had seized the throne from her son and caused his eyes to be stabbed out. She is said to have wanted to marry Charlemagne; but she could scarcely have helped him to adjudicate the morals of the Supreme Pontiff.

Since the problem could not be solved it was evaded. Charles conducted Leo back to Rome, where the Pope's oath of innocence was accepted by the clergy. And Leo then gave Charles the imperial crown. In later centuries both the spiritual and the temporal rulers could use this ambiguous exchange of favors to back their own claims to supremacy. But Charles himself was too busy with incessant wars to bother whether Popes created Emperors or Emperors created Popes.

He established Western Christianity in Germany, Bohemia, Austria, Croatia. He did his work so firmly that in the next century the Christian, Romanizing tide reached Poland and Hungary, leaving in Western Europe only Spain and Scandinavia to the infidel.

In every Christian (or ex-Christian) land where great poetry is revered and songs are sung, Charlemagne and his peers are deathless heroes. The people and the poets have thus shown their good sense. Charles had fought all his life — fifty-three campaigns in every corner of Europe — against the encircling pagans. He had built defensible boundaries. He had succeeded where Augustus failed, in fixing the frontier on the Elbe. Yet these were not wars of conquest in the name of security. They were wars to save the nascent West from annihilation. The barbarians attacked from eastern Germany, while northward the Viking storm was gathering. The Saracens held Spain and the African coast, and gained a foothold in Provence. Their pirates owned the Mediterranean Sea; Venetian trade with the Levant was strangled. The Franks and their religion were everywhere on the defensive.

These were not wars of murder in the name of Christ, but wars to prevent that name from being abandoned.

We may find a Christian symbolism in the fact that among the countless legends and epics celebrating Charles and his companions the most beautiful is a memorial to their one defeat,

> *dopo la dolorosa rotta, quando*
> *Carlo Magno perdè la santa gesta.*

There is no final triumph in this world, says Christianity. The pagans on the dark marches may be weakened for a time but they cannot be destroyed. Man is not good enough for success.

At the end of the *Chanson de Roland*, when peace has been made, and the traitor has been killed, and the Saracen queen has been converted and baptized, the great king lies down to sleep. At once God's angel appears and tells him to gather his armies for a forced march into a distant land where the besieged Christians implore his help. And the epic ends with three heart-moving lines: Charlemagne weeps and tears his white beard and cries to Heaven that his life is most painful and that he does not want this troublesome new mission. But we are left under no illusions: he will go where he is ordered, and fight for the old cause. He will win the mixed victory which is all that is allowed to man. His cares will never diminish until death. *

When Charlemagne at last found peace he too, like Gregory the Great, had earned the enduring gratitude of Christendom; but he had not built an enduring secular empire. His dominions were partitioned within forty years, and by 923 his family's power was ended. The crisis in the conflict between the new Western Empire and the Vatican, between Popes and Caesars, was postponed for two centuries — but the seeds had been planted on that famous Christmas Day in St. Peter's in the year 800.

* Li Emperere n'i volsist aler mie:
"Deus!" dist li Reis, "si penuse est ma vie!"
Pluret des oilz, sa barbe blanche tiret. . . .

(*Chanson de Roland*, 11, 3999–4001)

5

The main households of Charles the Great were established near the Rhine — including his favorite retreat at Aachen where he amused himself whenever possible with his fourteen children and his pet elephant named Abulabaz, the gift of Harun-al-Raschid. For the first time in the history of Europe the Rhine was the base for an empire, the center rather than the boundary. And although the Carolingian realm was soon undone the Carolingian notion of a state which should comprise all Western Christendom kept recurring in men's dreams.

In the tenth century Otto of Saxony united Central Europe from the Meuse to the Elbe, with Bohemia and Moravia as tributaries. In 951 he seized the crown of Italy. A few years later the Pope named him Emperor — but unhappily Otto's territories excluded France. If Charlemagne's wide conquests had been kept together, Western Europe might have been spared its most deadly division; but from the time of Otto the French and the Germans drew perilously apart. And the new Holy Roman Empire, shorn of France, wasted itself in the attempt to dominate the Papacy. From the moment Otto became emperor he tried to impose upon the Supreme Pontiff the yoke which the Byzantine Patriarch bore. The long medieval war between Guelphs and Ghibellines had begun. *

* The Oxford Dictionary believes that these mysterious words are corruptions of the German names *Welf* (the founder of the House of Brunswick and of the present dynasty in Great Britain) and *Wainblingen* (a Hohenstaufen estate in Germany). Others derive Guelph and Ghibelline from Arabian efforts to translate Hohenstaufen, or from the names of two contentious brothers in Pistoia. In any case, by the second half of the twelfth century in Italy, Guelphs were followers of the Popes, Ghibellines of the Holy Roman Emperors.

Otto deposed the very Pope who had crowned him, and substituted Leo VIII who recognized his right to veto papal elections. Soon the arrogant emperors were claiming that they themselves should name the Pope, and not merely reject an unsuitable choice. The distinction between God and Caesar, the basis of our civilization, might have been abolished. But at that point Hildebrand came upon the scene — a Tuscan peasant, brave, subtle, and farseeing, the third of the heroic figures who saved the youthful West from Eastern monism, from the state that gives orders to the Church.

First as Cardinal, and after 1073 as Pope Gregory VII, Hildebrand asserted the independence of the Vatican on all Church questions and the duty of the Vatican to see that the power of secular princes was justly used. The Popes, he said, should excommunicate and depose incapable monarchs and should confirm the choice of their successors. And in order to make the papal bureaucracy disciplined and fit for such duties he enforced the hated rule of celibacy upon his clergy. The West was to be a Christian commonwealth wherein the local rulers must observe the law of nations. And the Popes were to be the judges of such observance.

No compromise was possible between the pretensions of Hildebrand and those of the Holy Roman Emperors. The first clash came in 1075, when a Roman synod denied the right of any government in Europe to invest a prelate with the symbols of his office.

Henry IV, headstrong and young, had just succeeded to the Empire. He at once deposed the Pope, who replied by deposing and excommunicating the Emperor. The German princes deserted Henry, who was thus forced to make his famous penance before Hildebrand at Canossa. But as we said in Chapter One, Canossa did not end the conflict. The two implacable men were soon deposing each other again, this time in favor of an anti-Pope and an anti-King. Henry led four successive armies to the siege of Rome, and at last forced Hildebrand to flee. "I have loved justice and hated iniquity," were the Pope's final words, "therefore I die in exile." *

The "war of the investitures" was settled in 1122: the secular prince might exact homage for the temporal possessions of the Church, but could no longer invest with spiritual authority. In spite of this wise compromise the victory had clearly been Hildebrand's. He had purified the Church within and had made firm its moral rule. He had saved the Popes from what had seemed an inevitable servitude. And since his death in 1085, no absolute power has long survived in the West. No Tudor, no Bourbon, no Hapsburg or Hitler has silenced the recurring question: Is the state sovereign over the soul? Or is government merely "to serve and to keep order, not to dominate where it has no moral roots"?

Hildebrand, however, failed to save the Papacy "from the contagion of the world's slow stain." Freed from the Empire of their own rash reviving, the Popes quickly proved that they were by no means freed from original sin.

A hundred and five years after Gregory VII, on the eve of the thirteenth century, Innocent III raised the Papacy to the height of its power: the supreme authority in religious affairs, the supreme arbiter in temporal affairs. The Vatican became the court of last appeal against the oppressions of

---

* Dilexi justitiam et odivi iniquitatem: propterea morior in exilio.

princes. Innocent thought nothing of reprimanding the kings of England and France, to whom he wrote demanding peace. "It is bad for Christendom for Christian rulers to be at war," he told them. "We may not keep silent in such a necessity, like dumb dogs who cannot bark, lest the blood of so many of our people be required at our hands."

While chiding kings, the Pope gave aid to the exalted moral revivals of St. Francis and St. Dominic. But he also unhappily promoted the Fourth Crusade and the bloodthirsty war against the Albigenses. By the time of Innocent's death in 1216, Europe had learned that although a Pope might usefully keep watch over the secular watchmen he possessed no special grace helping him to keep watch over himself. Having escaped the imperial tyranny of Byzantium, Europe would not permit a theocratic tyranny in its place.

We have mentioned the disgrace that fell upon the Fourth Crusade, perverted from the redemption of the Holy Places to the theft of the Eastern Christian capital. Innocent was appalled by this dishonor, and gave orders that the conquered Greeks should not be coerced into the Western Church. Yet four years after the sack of Constantinople he turned his fierce crusaders against the heretical Albigenses of southern France. The consequent war of extermination lasted twenty-one years, ending in the peace of the graveyard.

Innocent had again been stricken with sorrow at his own handiwork. He had sought to turn the Albigensian Crusade away from France, toward the Muslims of Spain. He was too late. While the war still raged the disillusioned Pope died; but the civil strife within Christendom continued. By the middle of the thirteenth century Europeans were asking them-

selves the old Roman question: *Quis custodiet custodes?*
What good was a sacred authority, painfully preserved as
a court of appeal against the everlasting presumption of
princes, if that same authority were to start as many wars
as it suppressed, with no apparent knowledge of the dark
heart of man, and no power to control its own furious war-
riors?

Among the deeds which make his papal name seem only
too appropriate, Innocent III had unseated a Holy Roman
Emperor and had put in his place Frederick of Hohenstaufen,
Stupor Mundi, the Pope's own ward and the most brilliant
and ambitious of the medieval emperors. Frederick thus became the master of Sicily and Germany. As might have been
foreseen, he decided to become the master of Italy as well,
uniting his empire from the North Sea to the Carthaginian
straits. But the Papal States were in his way. Thus the
Emperor and the Pope, the two guardians of Christendom,
undertook to fight each other to the death. The crisis came
under Innocent IV, who finally destroyed Frederick — but
at the cost of destroying the last hope of a Christian Commonwealth. By the financial exactions that he laid upon all
Western peoples in order to fight his mundane war, he cooled
the affection and the sense of duty that had bound most
Europeans to the spiritual power of Rome.

At the dawn of the fourteenth century men knew that
neither the spiritual nor the secular power would unite the
West. The Hildebrandine hopes had faded. By promoting
German civil wars while Frederick was fighting in Italy the
Popes had made impossible an effective Empire in Central
Europe. German unity was sacrificed to the Guelph and

Ghibelline wars. By clinging to the Papal States at the cost of recurring conflict the Popes had sacrificed Italian unity as well, teaching the new city-states to conspire against each other with the suicidal persistence of the ancient Greeks.

Fifty years after the death of Innocent IV, a French king sent his envoy to kidnap the Pope. And Europe was not shocked. A few years later the French kidnaped not only the Pope but the whole Papal Government, and installed it at Avignon. After that Babylonian Captivity came the Great Schism of 1378–1417, when Europe abounded in Popes and anti-Popes. This was too much for men's loyalties. It was inviting the secular princes to step in and take for themselves the power that the Vicars of Christ were making ridiculous.

Toward the end of this dismal period Aretinus noted with surprise and shame that the Hobbesian fear — the dread of taking the first step toward peace — prevails even among Popes and anti-Popes. Describing the negotiations for Catholic reunion between the two remaining pretenders to the Papacy, he wrote: "If the one advances, the other retreats; the one appears an animal fearful of the land, the other a creature apprehensive of the water. And thus, for a short remnant of life and power, will these aged priests endanger the peace and salvation of the Christian world."

They had in fact destroyed the peace and unity of the Christian world. And for the time being they had destroyed the essential Christian dualism as well. The Great Schism, and the Great Cynicism which it promoted, led directly to the rebirth of the tyrant state.

6

In spite of their failings the men of the Middle Ages set the pattern for our civilization. The success of the West, in any period, must be measured by their standard of a law based on morals and not merely on the police, of a government which serves that law because it is true and which does not claim the power to veto it, and of an international community whose faith in the law transcends parochial boundaries.

The assertion of such a standard, in view of our perpetual failure to apply it, may seem boastful, unrealistic, a substitution of desires for facts. Yet it is a clear fact that we have always been aware of the standard, and that we like ourselves better when we are trying to live up to it than when we are not. Civilizations, like men and women, must have a moral purpose or die of sheer boredom — of that combination of weariness with self-disgust which Chaucer called *accidie* and to which Baudelaire gave the English name, spleen.

> *Rien n'égale en longueur les boiteuses journées*
> *Quand sous les lourds flocons des neigeuses années*
> *L'Ennui, fruit de la morne incuriosité,*
> *Prend les proportions de l'immortalité.**

* G. K. Chesterton says much the same thing in his more cheerful fashion: "Unless a man has a philosophy certain horrible things will happen to him. He will be practical; he will be progressive; he will cultivate efficiency; he will trust in evolution; he will do the work that lies nearest; he will devote himself to deeds, not words. Thus struck down by blow after blow of blind stupidity and random fate, he will stagger on to a miserable death with no comfort but a series of catchwords."

No glories of art or science, no military conquests, no mere wealth can sustain a civilization that has strayed from its own path. And the fruitful study of history becomes impossible if the nature of that path is ignored.

The Great Schism was followed appropriately by the Reformation, by the division of Christendom into warring sects. The Church had failed to preserve the moral unity of Europe, or the balance between government and religion. At first the Lutherans and Calvinists were as firm as the Roman Catholics that the Church should remain a separate authority, distinct from the state. But the Reformation was bound to make the Church subordinate — in Protestant countries and in Catholic.

The wealth of the clergy had long been envied by temporal princes who wished to seize all possible tax money for their own aggrandizement. The Papal court of last appeal, to which the oppressed might bring their grievances, was not only a nuisance to the oppressors when it found against them; it was also the richest court in Europe, since it lived on contributions from the entire West — and on the sale of indulgences, which drained the parishes of their spare cash.*

Thus the reformers found welcome support among kings and princes, and thus they became subject to the military power which protected them. They could not resist such power beyond the point of politeness, for if the protection were withdrawn they might be burned or imprisoned. Sin-

---

* The medieval kings regarded the sale of indulgences much as the British brewers of today regard the sale of television sets: the weekly or monthly installment payments have a bad effect on other business.

cere men, who at first wished only to make the Church more seemly and to restore it as the center of a Christian common- wealth, were led step by step into founding new churches, each of which was dependent on one of the rising national states. And the plunder of the old Church, now dispossessed, helped the national states to rise more rapidly and to become less amenable to moral pressure.

In the Catholic countries, meanwhile, Rome found herself ever more dependent on the temporal power; for if a king decided to suppress Protestantism in his realm he could first extort concessions from the Vatican. Soon all the Churches had an interest in preaching obedience, if not servility, to the state. Strong national states with obsequious national churches then plunged, as we have seen, into a century of religious warfare — culminating in the devastation of the Germanies between 1618 and 1648. The balance between Catholic and Protestant powers was so even that neither could reunite Christendom by force. All they accomplished was to dis- credit Christianity and to make men long for order even at the price of tyranny.

The Church, or Churches, could no longer afford pro- tection against the state, no longer insist on a distinction between the things that are God's and the things that are Caesar's. Yet the distinction remained, and Western man knew it. No sooner was he enslaved by the new despotisms than he began seeking a new defense for freedom. He found it, for the time being, in what we now call con- stitutional government. The state was to have limited powers, beyond which it must not move. The limitations were to be enforced by public opinion. Thus was the rule of law to be reborn in the name of Man, the name of God having proved unacceptable.*

7

The contrast between the revived despotisms, and the modern West which emerged after the American and French revolutions, may be seen by comparing the works of Thomas Hobbes with the Constitution of the United States. Hobbes, like Machiavelli before him, went beyond public opinion in his defense of pure power, in his assertion that the state can brook no moral restraint. But it was only the frankness of Hobbes that disconcerted his contemporaries. The doctrines, even when unacknowledged, were put into effect. The new national states practiced a revolutionary form of sovereignty, which ignored not only the Christian dualism but the ancient Western sense of unity. The dualism was soon restored, under secular sanctions; but the unity, to our disaster, still eludes us.

The medieval Popes and Emperors shared the widespread

---

* Molière's *Don Juan*, in 1665, gives one of the first clear statements of the new mood following the Thirty Years' War — so clear, indeed, that the passage was censored. Don Juan believes in nothing but the findings of arithmetic. He mocks the beggar who spends his time praying for other men, and suggests that he mind his own business and pray for a suit of clothes. He offers a louis d'or if the beggar will curse for a change; but when the Pauvre prefers to starve he relents: "*Va, va, je te le donne pour l'amour de l'humanité.*"

hopes for a Western commonwealth, however often they may have betrayed it. But the new Hobbesian states repudiated Europe, repudiated all obligations beyond their boundaries. The days of international anarchy had begun — the days of state idolatry. The full dangers of the new unbridled sovereignty were not clear until the boundless democratic enthusiasm was put behind these irresponsible centers of power. Then, in the twentieth century, the monsters who acknowledge no master began to fight each other to death. In the seventeenth century the monsters came bearing promises of order and efficiency. And the man who defended them most realistically, in all their nakedness, was Hobbes — who had learned his politics as secretary to Francis Bacon.

Leviathan was written in 1651, when the civil war in England had produced a dictatorship and the religious wars on the Continent had ended in wide ruin. Hobbes wanted security above all else. He believed that men use their reason chiefly for evil ends, and that their normal occupation, if allowed to go their own depraved way, is war. The natural state of man, with nothing but his strength and his invention to support him, is as bad as it could be, with "no knowledge of the face of the earth; no account of time; no arts; no letters; no society; and which is worst of all, continual fear, and danger of violent death; and the life of man, solitary, poor, nasty, brutish, and short."

To save him from his own horrid habits, man neeeds an absolute state. Whether it be headed by a king or an assembly does not much matter, but its powers must be all-inclusive and there must be no appeal from its rulings. Neither God nor conscience can be called upon for protection. The Church must be the servant of the state, whose powers are not only unlimited but perpetual. The state should control public opinion, for "the common people's minds are like clean paper, fit to receive whatsoever by Public Authority shall be printed upon them." There is no such thing as abstract justice. Morality, for the state, means doing what is expedient. And in any case tyranny is better than "that dissolute condition of masterless man, without subjection to laws, and a coercive power to tie their hands from rapine and revenge."

Here is the forecast of the totalitarian state, plus the calm indifferent acceptance of international anarchy. *Leviathan* does not even discuss the keeping of the peace between these demonic powers; in fact Hobbes accepts foreign war as a useful way of diminishing the population. "When all the world is overcharged with inhabitants," he writes, "then the last remedy of all is Warre, which provideth for every man, by Victory, or Death." Again — as in the aberrations of Stalin and Hitler — we find man considered as a brute. The state must be beastly because man is himself a jungle animal, fit only to be mastered and enslaved.

Yet a few years before the publication of *Leviathan*, in the midst of the hate-burdened Thirty Years' War, Grotius had written *De jure belli ac pacis* — proving once more that alongside man's lust for destruction dwells always the possibility of grace. Grotius hoped to diminish the savagery of Europe's self-slaughter by reviving the law of nature. That law would have validity, he boldly claimed, even if God did not exist. And like the laws of mathematics, it could not be repealed. He begged the proud leaders of the new unbridled states to take heed lest they destroy Society. All must perish, he said, in the international anarchy of their contriving. In self-preservation, governments must keep the law of nations and must combine against anyone who sought to break it. "The moment we recede from Right," he told the oblivious princes, "we can depend upon nothing." And he quoted Aristotle: "If faith be taken away all human correspondence ceases."

No arguments could halt Europe's drift toward despotism at home and lawlessness abroad. Emperor and Pope having failed to hold Christendom together, Grotius appealed to enlightened self-interest: the feeblest, the least inspiring, the most fitful of motives. When the nations chanced to be at peace, however, the new international rules proved useful. And Grotius was to become the father of many modern theories of natural law; but during his own lifetime the Thirty Years' War grew ever more furious, and Leviathan ever more insatiable.

The people of England, to be sure, were never wholly subjected by the Hobbesian state. Even the Tudor absolutism of the sixteenth century had been tempered by that astute family's feeling for public opinion. And after the Cromwellian wars and dictatorship, the restored monarchy admitted Parliament as a junior partner. By the end of the century, with the fall of the House of Stuart, the royal prerogative had been checked and balanced. A hook for Leviathan had been contrived, and a partial answer to the questions the Lord put to Job: "Will he speak soft words unto thee? Will he make a covenant with thee? Wilt thou take him for a servant forever?" The British people were on their way back toward the rule of law, at least in home affairs. But not so the people of the Continent.

The Hobbesian state flourished in Western Europe: absolute within, anarchic without. The purest and most powerful example was France, where the last words of Richelieu showed how far Europe had descended from the vision of Hildebrand. "Do you forgive your enemies?" was the conventional deathbed question. And the Cardinal answered, "I have no enemies but those of the state." In France, therefore, in the century after Richelieu, men turned in desperation toward the revived doctrines of natural law, and of the restraint upon arbitrary power which that law entails. The English had done the same during the Cardinal's lifetime, to justify their revolts against the Stuarts.

Natural law without a God, with nothing but a clockwork universe to sustain it, proved a difficult concept. We shall discuss later the efforts of the Enlightenment to find a moral force independent of religion, which would not only permit men to overthrow the tyrant state but which would support them in compelling the new "constitutional" governments to accept restricted powers. The generation of Thomas Jefferson believed the answer was obvious. Thus the West moved into the phase of self-limited governments. Power was to be controlled, and the old dualism restored, by the written or unwritten Constitution. The most dogmatic and the clearest example of the new system is found in the Constitution of the United States.

Hobbes had pronounced flatly that sovereign power must never be divided: "for what is it to divide the power of a commonwealth but to dissolve it; for powers divided mutually destroy each other." The makers of the American Constitution said that sovereignty must always be divided, since the alternative was the Hobbesian state, which was no fit habitation for man.

The Americans announced in their Declaration of Independence that men have inalienable rights with which no government may tamper. Yet they knew that most governments do tamper with these rights most of the time. Their task was to invent a government which could not do so — but which nevertheless could keep order, control foreign commerce, raise taxes, and protect the nation. They put their faith in the theory of "the balance of powers." They first divided sovereignty between the states and the federal government, and they then divided the powers of that government among the President, the Congress, and the Judiciary. Each, they hoped, would act independently and check the others, thus producing a total force too weak to destroy liberty. The whole elaborate mechanism, based largely on Montesquieu and Locke, was a substitute for the Church as a means of protecting man against the state.

At the convention that wrote the American Constitution James Madison was gloomily realistic. "In all cases where a majority are united by a common interest or passion," he said, "the rights of the minority are in danger. What motives are to restrain them? A prudent regard to the maxim, that honesty is the best policy, is found by experience to be as little regarded by bodies of men as by individuals. Respect for character is always diminished in proportion to the number among whom the blame or praise is to be divided. Conscience, the only remaining tie, is known to be inadequate in individuals; in large numbers little is to be expected from it." And on the same subject John Adams wrote: "Longitude and the philosopher's stone, have not been sought with more earnestness by philosophers than a guardian of the laws has been studied by legislators from Plato to Montesquieu; but every project has been found to be no better than committing the lamb to the custody of the wolf, except that one which is called a *balance of power*."

This revived dualism has proved insubstantial because of our failure to revive the sense of Western unity. The recent return of the grim Hobbesian state warns us that neither written nor unwritten Constitutions can maintain the rule of law in the face of our vast wars. The self-slaughter of the West in the twentieth century has been the chief cause of the new Leviathans. We seem to have forgotten that we once thought Christendom more important than any of its parts.

Is there no hope of restoring that lost brotherhood? Clearly we are no longer united by religion. Many of us feel like Molière's Don Juan: there is nothing true but arithmetic. Does that mean there is nothing to give character to the West, no common cause? Before accepting such pessimism let us review the history of natural law.

Chapter Four

☆   ☆   ☆   ☆   ☆

Natural Law

Chapter Four

But for natural law the petty laws of a small peasant community of peninsular Italy would never have become the universal law of an international civilization. But for natural law the great medieval synthesis of godly and of worldly wisdom would not have been possible. But for natural law there would probably have been no American and no French revolution, nor would the great ideals of freedom and equality have found their way into the law-books after having found it into the hearts of men.

A. P. D'ENTRÈVES

In 1903, at a conference of the Russian Social Democratic Party, a delegate asked whether man's basic civil liberties might be violated if the party leaders so ordered. "Yes," came the answer. Democracy, liberty, human rights: these were as nothing compared to the success of the revolution.

Lenin himself went further, both in theory and practice. He despised the bourgeois notion that men act on conscious beliefs which may be influenced by argument. Marx had "proved" that the opinions of most men are determined in advance, are "reflections" of the economic classes to which they belong. Trained Marxian revolutionists were thus the only people who understood history and who knew what must be done. Persuasion and discussion were a waste of time — the fatuity of liberals and intellectuals. The masses could only be saved by ruthless leaders. When saved, they would think what they were told. And they would be told what was appropriate to the new system.

M. Vishinsky put the same point briefly at the United Nations Assembly on 10 December 1948. "The rights of human beings," he said, "cannot be considered outside the prerogatives of governments, and the very understanding of human rights is a governmental concept." We are back in the ancient world, where "the passengers existed for the sake of the ship." Or we are back with Hobbes, who shocked John Milton by asserting that the minds of the common people "are fit to receive whatsoever by Public Authority shall be printed upon them."

This is the interesting difference between the West and Russia, and it is only accidentally allied to communism. No mere change in the methods of production could make men despise the souls of their neighbors. Neither Thomas Hobbes nor Machiavelli were communists; but they believed in absolute sovereignty, so they agreed perforce with M. Vishinsky. The agelong monism of Byzantium and Moscow made it easy for Russians to think that the people exist for the sake of the revolution.

A true Westerner might find the communist system of production desirable; but he could not find the Russian state desirable, for his tradition tells him that liberty is the highest political end. And the parent of liberty is our dualism. Western man lives in two societies, with divided loyalties, in a state of tension that has given our civilization its unique, its frightening, strength. Rival powers compete for our allegiance; we are forever straining to serve two masters. Our consequent dynamic energy is a source for that richness of individual character which has made the West great. But we shall defile the source if out of weariness or loss of faith we compose our ancient quarrel with this world by forgetting that we have also a duty to the next. The guardian of that duty is the natural law.

This is not something arbitrary, imposed by heaven amid thunder and lightening, as a task or a doom. It is the impulse within us to make our conduct conform to truth. It is the object and the motive of conscience. It is law because it is natural to man — to all of man. It shows the road to fulfillment. It is discovered, not invented, for it is built into the universe. We may ignore it but we cannot change it. No race conceivable to our minds would be exempt from it, and no political system. *Vox populi, vox Dei* is therefore misleading; for "the people" can no more alter natural law than can the Popes, or the tyrants, or the individual.

The whole of our creative literature — poetry, drama, fiction — has this law of nature behind it. The dilemmas and predicaments that the Western mind imagines are either in terms of this law and the temptations to evade it, or they are in terms of a mighty frustrate effort to deny what has so long seemed certain: *Phaedra*, for example, and *Faust*. Jean-Paul Sartre struggles against the natural law as ardently as Wordsworth upholds it. And every effort to escape from its ends in nihilism, cynicism, or plain despair; for man becomes less than man if he turns his back on it.

"The real perfection of all creatures is found in the prosecution and attainment of their respective ends. . . . " wrote Leo XIII. "From this it is manifest that the eternal law of

God is the sole standard and rule of human liberty, not only in each individual man, but also in the community. . . ."

Why is it "manifest"? Because without an eternal law, binding on the conscience, individuals cannot seek their respective ends, having no rights they can maintain against an earthly sovereign — not even the right to think minority thoughts, or to assemble for protest, or to be free from arbitrary arrest. Democracy may become as oppressive as tyranny, when natural law is denied. The Athenian democracy that condemned Socrates to death for his opinions, the French democracy that invented the Terror under which half mankind now cowers, the Senate of the United States that in spite of all the written "rights" of the Constitution degrades men's characters without due process of law, merely because they are suspected of unpopular ideas — all warn us that the People can be as dangerous as a Dictator if they fall into self-idolatry, forgetting that they are under a law not made by man. This is why we should never boast of our democracy to Russia or to Asian nations until we have made sure that the "will of the people" is bound and limited by sanctions that no Assembly can repeal. Here we are close to the heart of our faith, which alone can impose such sanctions. If we fall into confusion on this point the outside world may reasonably wonder whether the soul of the West is corroded.

2

Slightly below the summit of the highest of the Adirondack Mountains lies Lake Tear of the Clouds, the headwaters of the Hudson River. The stream which trickles from that improbable little pond, lost in the far silence, gathers volume throughout its course, becomes more man-polluted with every mile, and ends in the majestic river which made New York City possible — majestic, but soiled with garbage, industrial refuse, bilge water, and dead cats. Yet in spite of this dilution the Hudson keeps its quality. It is still, today, the reason for New York. If the topless towers were demolished, and if all who live in their shadow were vaporized simultaneously, the city would rise once more if the river remained.

Similarly, lost in the silence of time, the idea of a natural law was born of the Hebrew * and Greek genius in the morning of the world, when life seemed simpler if no less cruel. It too has gathered strength, as well as corruptions and impurities, during its long voyage. Because of the corruptions, many have sought to dispense with the tradition, which would be as unwise as dispensing with the Hudson River because of its stench, instead of straining out the refuse. The concept of a law that is independent of any sovereign, which cannot be repealed, which has a sanction that the state can neither give nor take away, is the rock on which our society rests.

The rights of conscience — which the Roman emperors,

* "The inspired men," wrote Lord Acton of the ancient Hebrews, "who rose in unfailing succession to prophesy against the usurper and the tyrant, constantly proclaimed that the laws, which were divine, were paramount over sinful rulers, and appealed from the established authorities, from the king, from the priests, and the princes of the people, to the healing forces that slept in the uncorrupted consciences of the masses."

with the approval of the classical world, denied to Christians — are secure only when men have a divided loyalty: to the government as a public utility, to the nation as a center of affection and memory, to the West as a close brotherhood of common tradition, to the human race as a brotherhood under God, to the Church (to their own souls, hearts, or inner lives) as a guide to what is right or wrong. When men refuse to let secular power deny these loyalties they have attained true liberty.

But they never do refuse unless they know that some things are eternally right, are not to be violated by the powers of this world.

Since man's reason is imperfect, and may be swayed by his physical and social environment, the "truths" which men "know" have been various and self-contradictory. The law of nature has been quoted for every cause, from that of Negro slavery in the United States to that of red revolution in Paris. And it has often shifted ground — or man's interpretation has shifted — on such thorny questions (for example) as private property.

Aristotle and many Roman jurists believed that property was "natural"; but the Stoics saw it as a necessary evil which must be endured but which did not form part of the eternal order. The early Christians followed the Stoics: property was a result of man's imperfection. It should be accepted regretfully, and society should take care that too much did not collect in too few hands.

By the thirteenth century the Church and the great monasteries were themselves wealthy, and the pessimism of the

Dark Ages in regard to this world had lifted. The secular order was no longer unimportant. Property was no longer a sign of the Fall, a product of man's weakness. For St. Thomas Aquinas as for Aristotle, private property was in accord with "nature." And although the Reformation brought vast transfers of property most of the new churches agreed with the old that this was a sound Christian institution.

Apologists for the English revolution of the seventeenth century, and for the American and French revolutions of the eighteenth, defended private property as a "natural right," and as a prerequisite to liberty. The propertyless man, they said, could not be truly free. Yet today we show signs of returning to the Stoic and the early Christian view that private property derives from man's sinfulness rather than from his rational nature, and that if it must be tolerated it should at least be kept strictly within bounds.

Such changes to and fro suggest that although the principles are clear we must not be too dogmatic about the details of natural law. "The notion," writes Professor d'Entrèves, "was laden with ambiguity even in the days when it was considered self-evident." The same is true of democracy, or of any word that has been used in many times and places. Partly because of this ambiguity we rejected democracy as a unifying concept for the West. Why, then, do we accept natural law?

The answer is simple. There is one constant and saving doctrine in all statements of natural law: the doctrine that the state may not coerce the conscience, may not require deeds of positive evil — not even war, if the conscience declares it unjust. And although the "eternal" law was different for Cicero, for Aquinas, and for Lincoln, two points should be remembered. First, even if men disagree from age to age on the "absolute" good, the conscience of each age should still be respected — else law degenerates into mere power, mere command. The state becomes as ruthless as Lenin; the citizen is "re-educated" until he thinks whatever is convenient. And second, the disagreements between Cicero and Aquinas, or Aquinas and Lincoln, are surprisingly few — and if the three men had been impossibly perfect there would have been no disagreements at all. "For the *divine* will, and in general for a *holy* will, there are no imperatives: *'I ought'* is here out of place, because *'I will'* is already of itself necessarily in harmony with the law."

Modern jurists enjoy scoffing at the "eternal truths" of natural law which never, they say, remain the same for two generations. The criticism should be leveled at man's frailty. Society changes; the means of production change; we face new conditions with rigid and outmoded customs, and we call upon the most sacred principles to justify our folly. Whatever this proves, it does not prove that right and wrong are the servants of an economic system.

The very meaning of "private property," for example, is forever shifting — which may explain our shifting judgment as to whether it is "natural." Spengler points out that "a writer like Cicero could never have conceived of 'intellectual property,' let alone property in a practical notion or in the potentialities of talent." Obviously, we should not confuse enduring truth with customs that must alter with every new invention. The natural law should be our standard for testing these customs and for rejecting those that have become unsuitable. When we use it as a defense of the indefensible we merely prove our own fallibility. We do not prove that moral values are relative.

A thorny problem arises when two groups in the same society disagree as to the higher law, and both turn to it for support. When this happened in France the law of nature was suddenly converted, as Lord Bryce said, into "a mass of dynamite which shattered an ancient monarchy and shook the European continent." This is what Jeremy Bentham meant when he wrote: "As to the Law of Nature . . . the natural tendency of such doctrine is to impel a man, by the force of conscience, to rise up in arms against any law whatever that he happens not to like."

We shall discuss later how the natural law came to be the excuse for the American and French revolutions; but here we must insist that Bentham exaggerated. It is only where positive law and morals intersect, and where positive law (the particular, temporary law of a state) interferes with the conscience and commands wrongdoing, that resistance is clearly justified. Most of the laws that rule the daily life of a community have nothing to do with morals, and those that have are mostly negative: they may be unjust, but they do not insist upon an act of sin.

Roman Catholics, for example, can live tranquilly in a state which permits free divorce. But if a mad tyrant decreed that all men must leave their wives every five years, and find new ones, these who held to the law of nature would resist. For the state, which should "serve and keep order," has no authority to destroy the family. The fact that it has the power is irrelevant. So long as the West survives, the resistance to a law that denies morals will be continual, and will in time triumph.

In 1922 Ernst Troeltsch, historian and theologian, spoke at the second anniversary of the German Hochschule für Politik. He told his fellow countrymen that ever since the late eighteenth century Germany had drifted from her faith in natural law and in the rights of man — "rights which are not the gift of the state, but the ideal postulates of the state, and indeed of society itself in all its forms." Germany had thus lost touch with the Western political tradition and had wandered vainly into a glorification of force. Troeltsch then outlined the history of natural law, and told his not-too-happy audience:

> We need not be astonished, therefore, to find that this system of ideas, with all its imperfections, and notwithstanding its divisions, was able to form a common front in the hour of need against German ideology, or that it could evoke, to meet the challenge of "German barbarism," the enthusiastic instincts of all who believed in universal ends common to all mankind — in Humanity, the cause of Natural Law, and the moral rules of Nature.

This is clearly an incomplete explanation of the First World War. Yet we may say that the wars which have dragged down the West since 1912 are in some part the result of a denial throughout the German world of the old doctrine of government as a servant — and a denial of the higher law without which that doctrine cannot be defended. If Troeltsch had lived to see the second war, and the secession of many Westerners to Stalinism, he would not have revised his statement of our true political tradition.

3

The Greek mind saw the strength and beauty of "universal ends common to all mankind" as early as the sixth century B.C. "He who speaks with understanding must take his foothold on what is common to all," wrote Heraclitus of Ephesus, "even more firmly than the city stands on the foothold of law; for all human laws are nourished by the divine law." Socrates in the next century taught his disciples to judge of right and wrong, not in terms of power or expedience, but by the light of a God-given reason and conscience. He did not call for resistance to evil laws; but at least he set men free to criticize.

Plato went further. Appalled by the excesses of Greek democracy he taught that the will of the people must bow before the divine rules of justice, and that the authority of any city (except his own dream-Republic) was similarly limited. No one has stated more beautifully the need to judge the powers of this world by a standard from heaven.

In the fourth century Aristotle explained natural law more systematically, although for him as for Socrates it remained

an ideal rather than a practical hope. He said there were two
sorts of law:

> the particular and the universal. *Particular* law is the law
> defined and declared by each community for its own mem-
> bers. . . . Universal law is the law of nature. . . . There
> really exists, as all of us in some measure divine, a natural
> form of the just and unjust which is common to all men,
> even when there is no community or convenant to bind
> them to one another. It is this form which the Antigone
> of Sophocles' play evidently has in her mind, when she says
> that it was a just act to bury her brother Polynices in spite
> of Creon's decree to the contrary — just, she means, in the
> sense of being *naturally* just.

M. Jacques Maritain calls Antigone "the eternal heroine of
the natural law." Her story is the supreme expression of
man's revolt against the perversion of authority, and of man's
faith in that law of right which the Greeks, from Heraclitus
to Aristotle, splendidly affirmed. Antigone died, not seeking
privilege or benefits for herself, but refusing to obey a law
that commanded her to do wrong. When the tyrant Creon
decided that her brother's body should be left to the dogs
and the birds, desecrated and deprived of the last rites, he
committed an unnatural deed of horror. And when he
argued that he could not pardon Antigone because the law
is the law and must be obeyed, he raised the most important
question in politics: Is it the law because Power says so? Or
because it is right?

"How dared you break my command?" asked Creon; and
Antigone answered with the words that have made her immortal:

> *I did not rate*
> *Thy proclamations for a thing so great*
> *As by their human strength to have overtrod*
> *The unwritten and undying laws of God:*
> *Not of today nor yesterday, the same*
> *Throughout all time they live; and whence they came*
> *None knoweth. How should I through any fear*
> *Of proud man dare to break them and then bear*
> *God's judgment?*

From this no threats can move her. She repeats it in her last cry when the Guards take her, terrified but unyielding, to her doom:

> *Oh, of our Princes is there one who sees*
> *Me, the great King's last daughter, deathward driven. . . .*
> *Because I am faithful to the Laws of Heaven.*

Some modern commentators on natural law, who see it merely as a body of sensible rules for civilized life, and who deny it a larger sanction, have sought to show that Aristotle was of their view. Why, then, did he mention Antigone? Why did he "fly to the will of God" * as soon as he spoke of the higher law? There is no ambiguity about that tragic princess. She walks untimely to her grave because she knows that it accords with the divine will to honor the dead. "Enlightened self-interest" would not have taught her that she must die. Common sense would have whispered to leave her brother's corpse rotting on the battlefield, with no libations poured; but she could not. Where should one learn such

---

* Cf. page 13.

behavior if there is no truth? In whose name do we defy the tyrant's laws, if there are no others?

Antigone's sister, Ismene, was too timorous to help bury Polynices. Yet later she claimed to have taken part in the "crime," and she demanded the death sentence:

> *Sister, reject me not. Oh, take me too*
> *To die with thee and give the dead his due.*

She was ashamed to live, ashamed to have it said that she obeyed the voice of Creon rather than the voice of God. She would die dishonored if she survived her sister: "homeless on earth, homeless among the dead." In the character of this terrified girl Sophocles displays the power of a moral concept to strengthen our frail flesh. And throughout he warns that goodness does not bring happiness here on earth. Those who serve God's Laws, he says, are more likely to suffer than to be rewarded. Antigone died because it was her duty; but she died miserable and afraid:

> *Alone, alone,*
> *Unwept, unfriended, with no escort song,*
> *They lead me. All is ready for the long*
> *Road that is all my own.*

4

The three generations of the Socratic school did more for the future reign of the people than all the institutions of the States of Greece. They vindicated conscience against authority and subjected both to a higher law; and they proclaimed that doctrine of a mixed constitution which has prevailed at last over absolute monarchy and still has to contend against extreme Republicans and Socialists and against the masters of a hundred legions.

On the threshold of the Christian era the Stoic philosophers went one step further. They said that all men are born free and equal, citizens of a universal commonwealth, children of God, bound in charity to each other. The Stoics were the first to dare imagine a universal Church, superior to any sovereign. Unhappily, they did not change the politics of Rome. Men had to build a state that was not absolute before they could hope for a justice that might prevail.

Natural law for the Romans was still a plan of perfection that no one sought seriously to impose upon the ugly facts of life. The natural was what "ought to be": but few foresaw the demand that it should be made to coincide with "what is." The natural was the higher law, the justice that never could prevail until the authority of the state was limited by a force outside the state. So the Stoics, who had seen the truth, could only advise their disciples to flee the life of politics and power and to practice virtue silently.

A new dispensation became possible when men spread abroad the answer that our Lord made to the questions of the Pharisees and the Herodians: "Master, we know that thou art true, and carest for no man: for thou regardest not the person of men, but teachest the way of God in truth: Is it lawful to give tribute to Caesar, or not? Shall we give, or shall we not give?" The words with which Christ replied, as Lord Acton says, gave to the civil power, under the protection of conscience, a sacredness it had never enjoyed, and bounds it had never acknowledged; and they were the repudiation of absolutism and the inauguration of freedom. For our Lord did not only deliver the precept, but created the force to execute it. To maintain the necessary immunity in one supreme sphere, to reduce all political authority within defined limits, ceased to be an aspiration of patient reasoners, and was made the perpetual charge and care of the most energetic institution and the most universal association in the world.

5

We saw in the last chapter that "the most universal association in the world" did not contrive to reduce political authority — or even its own authority — to defined limits. Success is not within man's grasp; but at least the medieval purpose was clear, and out of it was born the West. So long as it remains clear the West will survive.

And let us forever do honor to our Graeco-Roman ancestors by recalling our debt to their concept of the law. Here was the basis for a Christian political theory that was lacking in the Gospels. The words of our Lord gave the precept for a division of Church from state. The centuries of Greek and Roman thinking on the nature of law showed how it might be done.

Yet when Cicero, under Stoic influence, writes that God is the author of the eternal law we are left wondering what he means, for he too fails to suggest that this law should overrule the laws of the state. He says "it is a sin to try to alter this law." But politicians are accustomed to sins; they can only be restrained by a sanction stronger than rhetoric.

The same perplexity strikes us when we read in the *Institutes* of Justinian that "the laws of nature . . . remain always stable and immutable, enacted as they are by the very Providence of God." For these laws, according to the Stoics, decree equality, freedom, religious toleration, self-denial and self-sacrifice, the forgiveness of our enemies, the willingness to suffer injustice but not to commit it. If in fact they came from God, it would seem that the Roman state and the Roman society required overhauling. We almost expect a Jeffersonian protest in the name of "the rights of man" — or a William H. Seward in the Forum Romanum, denouncing slavery because it violates "the higher law."

The expectation is vain. Nothing in the Justinian codes asserts that natural law can overrule the law of the community, or that freedom of conscience is any lively concern of the Roman state. If the lawyers of Byzantium may be judged by their great surviving handiwork, they merely quoted phrases from the Stoics to make clear that law *should* correspond to equity and justice. They did not claim that this was a fact. They did not claim that if the law was wicked the people had a right to change it or to ignore it. They meant, it seems, that the law should be as close to what is "natural" as the exigencies of the state permitted: wherever possible it should be based on universal principles.

This was no small bequest to posterity. A system of law

which sought to be valid for the wide Empire, and which admitted that the true standard was what man's conscience knew to be right, was a priceless gift to the West. The vision of the Roman jurists has never been forgotten. Their partial success in their high aim still gives romance and glory to the memory of the Roman Wall within which the law prevailed: "mile upon mile, from snow to desert, a single great girdle round the civilized world . . . and along the wall the armed might of the Empire, sleepless, holding the line."

When the Wall had been abandoned, and the West had emerged from the calamities and the pessimism of the Dark Ages, natural law was reaffirmed, shorn of its old ambiguity. It was no longer a vague ideal, powerless and largely disregarded; it was a duty to be enforced upon the state. As early as the twelfth century we find Gratian writing, "Natural law absolutely prevails in dignity over customs and constitutions. Whatever has been recognized by usage, or laid down in writing, if it contradicts natural law, must be considered null and void." At last we know exactly what is meant: God is truth, and the law which stems from His will must override the customs and constitutions of man. If we read Cicero from a Christian point of view he seems to be saying the same thing; but to the pagan mind he was expressing a theory, not a fact. With Gratian we have moved into a world where the rights of conscience, the freedom to do what is necessary for salvation, can be asserted against the state.

Thomas Aquinas said that man has "a certain share in the divine reason itself, deriving therefrom a natural inclination to such actions and ends as are fitting. This participation in the Eternal Law by rational creatures is called the Natural law."

The Eternal law, for Aquinas, was the full mind of God, which man could not hope to know. Divine law was that part of the mind of God which was revealed in the Bible or communicated through the Church. Natural law was that part of the mind of God which man could discover through his own reason. Last of all came human law — the laws of the state. And he agreed with Gratian that "all humanly enacted laws are in accord with reason to the extent that they derive from the natural law. And if a human law is at variance in any particular with the natural law, it is no longer legal, but rather a corruption of law." And he adds — which would have horrified the pagan world — that man is only bound to obey secular rulers "to the extent that the order of justice requires."

Again we seem to hear the voice of Jefferson; but again we must beware. If possible Jefferson was even farther from Thomas Aquinas than from Justinian. Natural law to the Middle Ages was not a statement of "rights," an excuse for a Whig revolution. It was a standard by which government could be judged; but it was also a promise that government would be worthy of respect.

In the Dark Ages many Christians had thought the state incorrigible, scarcely worth discussing. "What does it matter to man," said St. Augustine, "in this brief mortal life, under whose rule he lives, provided the rulers do not force him to do evil?" The Vandals were then at the gates of his

North African town, which they sacked the year of his death. The Roman world had been a long time dying; but the end was near — and Augustine's pupil, Gregory the Great, had not yet given hope that a new world might arise. Thus many of the early Christians, like the Stoics of old, thought natural law could be honored only in private, by a man who had fled society.

The high Middle Ages — the twelfth and thirteenth centuries — knew no such pessimism. The principles of justice they said, were known to man through the natural law, and might one day prevail through the Christian commonwealth. Imperfection, however, was to be expected from fallen man, and there should be neither vain repining nor insubordination if in secular matters the state made cruel mistakes. But if a prince dared to deny freedom of conscience, or to make war on fellow Christians for motives that were wholly evil, the Church would hold him to account. If he persisted in sin the Church would absolve his subjects from the duty of obedience; otherwise she would support authority.

The state was no longer an enemy. It was a servant of the Christian commonwealth. The words of our Lord had given to the Civil power "a sacredness it had never enjoyed," as well as "bounds it had never acknowledged." The natural law for the Middle Ages was a source of harmony between the values of this world and of the next. It made for conservatism, not for Jeffersonian revolt.

The distinction between natural law as an excuse for revolution, and natural law as the bond of society, becomes clear if we consider the "abolitionists" who helped precipitate the

American Civil War. The abolitionists hated Negro slavery for moral reasons. Their appeal was to Jefferson's Declaration of Independence, which was based upon the higher law, and to the Christian doctrine of man's brotherhood. The appeal was valid: all the heroes of natural law have taught that it annuls slavery. Yet a major question remained: Was slavery so deep an evil that it canceled all other political rights and interests? Was the Union itself insignificant compared with this vast wrong? Must the latest-born and most hopeful of political experiments die? Some of the best men in America welcomed a dissolution. "I do not see," said Ralph Waldo Emerson, "how a barbarous community and a civilized community can constitute one state." Surely the adjectives are insensitive? Emerson was comparing Massachusetts with Virginia, not Paradise with a concentration camp.

Such self-righteousness is likely to afflict men who claim too detailed a knowledge of God and of His judgments. This is a trap which the doctrine of natural law sets for the unwary. The principle, in Emerson's case, was clear and undeniable: good men should work for the freedom of the slaves. But what made Emerson so sure that the South was barbarous, or that the way to break slavery was to break the Union? "The achievement of a decent measure of honesty in our judgment of our fellow men," writes Reinhold Niebuhr, "and in our estimate of the meaning of the human drama in which we are involved is . . . something else than a mere intellectual achievement. It is a religious achievement which requires that the human tendency to claim a final position of judgment, though we are interested participants of the drama, must be overcome." We can be positive, in other words, about the principles of truth and justice proclaimed by the higher law. We cannot be positive about our own fumbling application of those principles. Our judgment will be warped by prejudice and weakened by ignorance.

Lord Acton, commenting on the American abolitionists, took a more cautious and less stirring stand than Emerson:

> [The Church's] system of Christian liberty is essentially incompatible with slavery; and the power of masters over their slaves was one of the bulwarks of corruption and vice which most seriously impeded her progress. Yet the Apostles never condemned slavery even within the Christian fold. The sort of civil liberty which came with Christianity into the world, and was one of her postulates, did not require the abolition of slavery. If men were free by virtue of their being formed after the image of God, the proportion in which they realised that image would be the measure of their freedom. Accordingly, St. Paul prescribed to the Christian slave to remain content with his condition.

Here is a proof that the concept of natural law, bequeathed to us by the ancient world, gave a basis for mundane political justice which is not found in the Gospels. The New Testament could make terms with slavery in this life; but the law of nature could not. And Acton's reference to St. Paul is doubly interesting, for this is the passage to which Marxists appeal when they denounce Christianity as the opium of the masses.

> Let every man abide in the same calling wherein he was called. Art thou being a servant? care not for it: but if thou mayest be made free, use it rather. For he that is called

in the Lord, being a servant, is the Lord's freeman: likewise also he that is called, being free, is Christ's servant. Ye are bought with a price; be not ye the servants of men. Brethren, let every man, wherein he is called, therein abide with God.

An American abolitionist in the eighteen-fifties, if he did not believe in the next world, must have been irritated by such talk. If equality in heaven was to him an idle dream, he could at least insist that the Negro should not be insulted on earth. And if this world was indeed the end of the story, there was perhaps no time to wait. But if the slave was "the Lord's freeman," if he had an immortal soul and was not prevented from seeking salvation, wise men might be willing to postpone the day of his liberation rather than to foment secession or civil war. But for those who followed the law of nature, it could only be a postponement.

This patience in the face of recalcitrant fact was Abraham Lincoln's policy. But Lincoln was aware that "the dense web of the fortunes of man is woven without a void." He did not flatter himself that the severing sword could cure one problem without creating others just as odious. Neither did he flatter himself that the sword could therefore remain forever sheathed. He knew that some principles must be defended even if frustration were foredoomed; but he could not fall into the self-righteousness of Emerson, because he knew that in the act of fighting for the good he was certain to provoke much evil. "Although there is a necessity in common principle," wrote Aquinas, "the more we descend to the particular the more we encounter defects."

6

Virtue is reason, said Plato on many occasions. And the Middle Ages agreed that reason is the divine spark in man: by the light of reason he can tell good from evil. Thus he can take part in God's plan. And thus, to the mind of the thirteenth century, he could attain dignity and participate in glory. Knowing the truth through his reason, and being helped to serve it by his Church, he could aspire to build a just society. "It is the task of Justice," wrote Aquinas, "to draw to equality those who are unequal: the work of justice has been fulfilled when this equality has been achieved." We are back with the Stoics, or forward with Jefferson. For pagan, for Christian, or for post-Christian, the law of nature teaches the equality of men.

Ambiguity returns, however, when the friends of natural law say that no human laws are binding if they contradict the universal. For the Stoics, the statement meant that the virtuous man must withdraw from this contaminated world; for Aquinas it meant that unless the Pope loosed the bonds of allegiance the government must be treated with reverence; for Jefferson it meant permission for revolution. Yet here, in this perplexing and sometimes obscure notion of a final allegiance to the absolute, we see why Sir Frederick Pollock sought to bring the common law of England into the great tradition. The fathers of the common law, wrote Pollock, "were making right and wrong for us and for our children."

Henry of Bracton, one of the thirteenth-century fathers, taught that the King is under God and law — that law is not command, but the rule of reason. We have seen that Christopher St. German in the sixteenth century agreed with Bracton and with Pollock, for he described the law of nature as "the law of reason as it is commonly called by those that are learned in the law of England." Hence the statement of the great Sir Edward Coke, so dear to the American colonists who made the revolution of 1776: "it appears in our books that in many cases the common law will control acts of Parliament and sometimes have judged them to be utterly void." Although this dictum is no longer part of the British Constitution, woe to the Parliament which takes advantage of its powers and disregards the common law.

The medieval English had turned their backs on the rigid, formalized Justinian Code (and on the Canon Law which they mistrusted as an excuse for foreign meddling) and had invented their own practical, pragmatic system. But "the law of nature was throughout the creative centuries of the common law a familiar idea and a guiding principle among lawyers and judges. In the philosophy of the common law the end of man is not among finite things. The moral and spiritual life of man is accordingly independent of the state authority."

Sir Thomas More said upon the scaffold: "I die the King's good servant, but God's first." However "God" may be interpreted today — even if His existence be denied — there speaks the West. "The King's good servant" — but the King may not give orders to the conscience.

"Think not that morality is ambulatory," wrote Sir Thomas Browne, "that vices in one age are not vices in another, or that virtues, which are under the everlasting seal of right reason, may be stamped by opinion." Long after it had become fashionable to make fun of the ambiguities of natural law, the old unconquerable faith was restated in every age. "A sound political morality," wrote Goldwin Smith in the nineteenth century, "will sanction strong measures in evil times; selfish ambition, treachery, murder, perjury, it will never sanction in the worst of times, for these are the things that make times evil — Justice has been justice, mercy has been mercy, honor has been honor, good faith has been good faith, truthfulness has been truthfulness from the beginning."

These obvious yet profound statements are the recurrent answer of the West to Hobbes, who says "it is not wisdom but authority that makes a law" — or to Oliver Wendell Holmes, who says it is not wisdom but majority opinion that determines truth. Are they not also the last, best answer to the idolatry of the Third Rome?

Chapter Five

*   *   *   *   *

Nationalism versus Natural Law

Chapter Five

Ni l'Ordre ni l'Etat ne vous appartiennent. Ils sont le legs de ceux qui ne sont plus, le patrimoine de ceux qui ne sont pas encore. Ce n'est pas votre maison que vous habitez, c'est la maison commune, bénie par le Christ. Si vous la démolissez sous pretexte d'ensevelir sous les decombres ceux qui la pillent, où coucheront donc vos enfants?

GEORGES BERNANOS

WHEN ANTIGONE first confessed her brave design, her sister recoiled. "We are subjects," said the awe-struck Ismene,

*and must needs obey our king
In this, aye or in many a bitterer thing.*

Such was the view of Hobbes, and of King Creon himself: law is power, and there can be no appeal. Oliver Wendell Holmes put the case bluntly: "As long as law means force — (and when it means anything else I don't care who makes it and will do as I damn choose) — force means an army. . . ." In his old age he expressed the same thought more subtly. "I can imagine a book on the law," he wrote to Pollock when he was ninety-one, "getting rid of all talk of duties and rights — beginning with the definition of law in the lawyer's sense as a statement of the circumstances in which the public force will be brought to bear upon a man through the

157

Courts. ... " But the "lawyer's sense" is deficient even in the courtroom; for what becomes of it when the public force is brought to bear in vain?

Holmes was a soldier in the American Civil War. During his boyhood he must have seen the mobs of Boston impeding the arrest of fugitive slaves, or setting the slaves free after they had been taken. Ninety years earlier he would have seen similar mobs in all the coastal towns preventing the "stamp masters" from administering an act of Parliament. Was the stamp tax a law in Boston? Was the Fugitive Slave Act? The lawyers, in each case, could state the circumstances in which force would be brought to bear; but only the conscience of the public could tell whether the force would operate.

Sir Frederick Pollock was more realistic when he wrote: "Law, on the whole, expresses the common conscience of those who are subject to it. If it did not, it would not be obeyed, at least in a free country." Or even in a tyrant state, we might add, if the state contained many subjects like Antigone. Creon had a good army, which had just won a large war, yet his "law" did not prevent the burial of Polynices. Modern tyrannies, to be sure, are more efficient. We may fairly say that in the land of a Hitler or a Stalin "law means force"; but it seems wayward to pretend that the words are adequate for the free West.

When we leave the police court and the classroom, "law in the lawyer's sense" is unrewarding, and "getting rid of all talk of duties and rights" is banal. We need something that will lift our souls to grandeur if we are to preserve any part of our globe for freedom — and we find it in the old statement that law is *not* command, but justice and the rule of reason. If we are asked who makes this law and who supports it, we can give one of two answers. We can say with Antigone and with the schoolmen that it represents what we can grasp of "the unwritten and undying laws of God." Or we can say with Grotius that it is so woven into the nature of things, like the laws of mathematics, that God himself cannot repeal it.

If we make the second choice, and if subsequently we cease to believe in God, we shall understand the concept of natural law that flourished in the eighteenth century.

2

We have seen that in the midst of the Thirty Years' War, when the national states that had risen from the wreck of Christendom were torturing Europe, Grotius sought to build a law of nations upon the tradition of natural law. Thus he challenged the doctrine of absolute sovereignty — that deadly concept revived from the ancient world.

At the moment when the people of England were contriving "a hook for Leviathan" in their own domestic politics, Grotius sought to fasten a similar restraint upon the huge anarchic beast in its relation with other states. While Cardinals and Ministers were flattering tyrants with the "divine right of kings," Grotius not only reaffirmed that natural law is a moral code which man can discover by the use of his reason, and which may not be repealed by any power, but he added that it is as binding abroad as at home, in foreign as in domestic relations, and that it is so clearly a part of the structure of the universe that it would remain valid even if God did not exist, or did not care.

None of these four statements was new to Christian thought; but by combining them Grotius became the father of the secular theory of natural law, in which God is gradually pushed aside to be replaced by an earthly sanction. This would have shocked the pious Dutchman, who had merely written (perhaps with the impious monarchs in mind) that "what we have been saying would have a degree of validity even if we should concede that which cannot be conceded without the utmost wickedness, that there is no God, or that the affairs of men are of no concern to Him."

Even more shocking to Grotius would have been the total failure of his international law to diminish aggression, or to limit the "just wars" which might still have to be fought against aggressors. In the latter field he had a brief success. But in his primary aim he could do nothing.

"The solid scholar," writes John Bowle, "with his method and erudition, looking out from his study, as from some calm Dutch interior, thought to establish European order out of the calculated aggression, the deadly cunning, the swift violence, of the rulers of seventeenth-century France, out of the bouncing militarism which was to culminate in the campaigns of Condé and Turenne." In that fierce world Grotius predicted that war might ruin Europe as it had ruined the liberties of the classical culture. He pleaded for an understanding that true law is independent of force, that it teaches good faith and points the way toward justice even if no armies are behind it. *Pacta sunt servanda* was the foundation of his law of nations. It may one day serve as an appropriate inscription upon the tombstone of our society.

The failure of Grotius may seem to justify the sardonic skepticism of Holmes; but that way lies death. We have seen in our own time wars more terrible and states more demonic than those of the seventeenth century. Let us be warned. Instead of repudiating Grotius, let us take up his work where he was forced to leave it. Realism concerning the nature of man, and his colossal wickedness, need not lead to despair, for man's gifts are equally great in both directions. "He is born capable of more good and more evil than the Moralists could ever imagine, for he was not created in the image of the Moralists, but in the image of God."

Nevertheless, the world of seventeenth-century politics was a hard world for those who tried to nurture the goodness in their neighbors' hearts. "When the last of the Reformers died," writes Lord Acton, "religion, instead of emancipating the nations, had become an excuse for the criminal art of despots." In such a Europe, where the writ of the Church no longer ran, where the Holy Roman Empire had failed as an alternative bond of union, where the new national states admitted no superiors and served no god but self-interest, the despots were bored at hearing that a higher law commanded respect for treaties. But the despots were transient; they did not hold the future of the West in fee. The men of the new age were pleased to agree with Grotius that reason, without revelation and without the help of God, could unfold ultimate truth. These were the men of science, and the philosophers of the Enlightenment, who were about to build the modern world.

3

We have said that the concept of the rule of law led to the Christian dualism. The same concept gave justification to the men who destroyed the unity of the Church, on the ground that the Church had broken the law. And now that concept was to make possible the scientific revolution. An idea that had long been implicit in the mind of Western man became explicit, and changed the face of the globe: the idea that every observable phenomenon in nature was also evidence of an immutable law which man was capable of discovering.

The revolution began with the oldest of the sciences: mathematics, astronomy, and the study of motion or inertia. No break in the close web of history occurred; yet the seventeenth century was a time of violent transition. The assertion of absolute sovereignty, the transfer of power from the Mediterranean to the north of Europe, the radical secularization of thought, the promotion of the natural sciences above philosophy and theology as a guide to truth; all this had long been preparing underground, but in the seventeenth century it came to the surface.

Toward the end of that century Malebranche could still write: "It is legitimate to regard astronomy, chemistry, and almost all the other sciences as suitable diversions for a decent man," but we "should not be dazzled by their brilliance or put them before the science of man himself." But Malebranche was a Catholic priest and he spoke for an older world — like Pascal, who at the age of thirty-one turned from mathematics and physics, in which he had shown genius, and retired to the Jansenist abbey of Port Royal to spend his life in the service of the faith. This is a point of view which will always recur; but no one would call it typical of the new West that was emerging while Malebranche wrote and while Pascal sought solitude.

Isaac Newton, one of the fathers of the modern dispensation, was a man of religion. He sought God's handiwork in mathematics and aspired to show the beauty, symmetry, consistency, of the divine order. He distrusted the clockwork exactitude of the world Descartes was contriving, which needed a God to wind the clock but for no other purpose. This distrust was quickly justified. The "methodical doubt" * of Descartes was vulgarized: the clock remained, but the Winder was forgotten. Not the humble men of science, but the self-confident *philosophes*, set the course for Western civilization. And in so doing they found the natural law of Grotius almost as useful as the mechanical law of Newton. In fact they very nearly succeeded in merging them.

* "Pour atteindre à la vérité," wrote Descartes, "il faut une fois dans sa vie se défaire de toutes les opinions que l'on a reçues et reconstruire de nouveau, et dès le fondement, tous les systèmes de ses connaissances."

Although the schoolmen of the Middle Ages had made large claims for reason, insisting that by reason alone man could learn right conduct and the law of nature, they also taught that the Bible and the Church were the guides to Divine Law — to that part of the mind of God which man could not reach unaided. This distinction was abandoned gradually, almost imperceptibly, by the prophets of the eighteenth century. Dazzled by the success of the natural sciences, men came to think of Nature and God as almost interchangeable terms.

The way to know God, according to the new teachers, was to study the mechanism of the world He had created, not the words of His Apostles or of His Church. The men of science were uncovering new "laws of the universe" every day. Why should they not in time (and in a very short time, thought the eighteenth century) uncover them all? The mind of God would then stand fully revealed to human reason. Natural law and the Divine Law would be merged. There would be no more mysteries. Human ignorance (an unhappy product of religious obscurantism) would be finally overcome.

Little by little, as this complacency grew, we find God receding into the background with the other mysteries. No one yet wished to abolish Him; but He did not seem as necessary as of old. He reappeared occasionally as the Final Cause, the Prime Mover, or the Great Contriver: the Being who wound up the clock and then forgot it. Jefferson expressed the new mood when he wrote that "the Laws of Nature and of Nature's God" entitled the American people to leave the British Empire. The two laws have been merged: they can both be discovered in the mind of man. "Having deified Nature," writes Carl Becker, "the eighteenth century could conveniently dismiss the Bible."

When the new self-confidence was carried into the realm of human relations the results were interesting. Men now declared that it was possible, by the use of reason, to bring all mundane institutions into harmony with the Universal Order. The total will of God, or of the Prime Mover, was revealed in the book of nature, and man had at last cast off his dark glasses and begun to read the book. Needless to say, John Locke had only to read a few pages to find that the will of God was expressed in the Glorious Revolution of 1688. Jefferson and his friends had only to read a few more to find the same approval for the Revolution of 1776. James Wilson, for example, wrote that "the happiness of the society is the first law of every government. This rule is founded on the law of nature." And Madison refers to "the transcendant law of nature and of nature's God, which declares that the safety and happiness of society are the objects at which all political institutions aim." (Neither Madison nor James Wilson felt that the British Parliament was aiming with sufficient accuracy.)

Similarly, the French had only to refer to the reliable book to find a happy concord between the law of nature and that "Declaration of the Rights of Man and of the Citizen" which they adopted in 1789. By this time, writes Professor d'Entrèves, "What Grotius had set forth as a hypothesis has become a thesis. The self-evidence of natural law has made the existence of God perfectly superfluous."

The old doctrine, which drove the Stoics into proud withdrawal, and which in the Middle Ages was a bond between the City of Man and the City of God, had become a doctrine of revolution. Yet the continuity is clear: man still appealed from the unjust laws of society to the law which is founded on reason and conscience. In the classical world he appealed in silence, uplifting his private conduct but making no complaint, since the state was omnipotent and owned the Church. In the Middle Ages he appealed through the intervention of the Church, an autonomous power. In the modern West, where conscience is free but no Church can mediate with a sovereign state, he appeals through constitutional channels if they are accepted — and if not, he appeals through force.

When natural law ceased to be a partial knowledge of the mind of God which must be supplemented by Church and Scriptures, when it boasted a final unqualified knowledge of man's "rights," it became the philosophy of revolt — and under the guise of the "rights of man" it became the religion of the Enlightenment. As such, it became also the whipping boy for the new idolatrous nationalism.

4

The American Revolution was the turning point. We have too long looked upon 1789 as the year of the great transition, when the West began to rebuild from its political foundations. Yet 1789 might have been impossible but for 1776. The Americans made revolution seem respectable, even reasonable. They were backed (selfishly, to be sure) by monarchies in Europe, and by many of the most careful thinkers in England. They built a democracy that seemed to have learned the sad lessons of classical history and of the Italian city-states — a democracy vigilant against its own excesses, which respected liberty and distrusted the tyranny of numbers. "Ancient Europe opened its mind to two new ideas — that Revolution with very little provocation may be just; and that democracy in very large dimensions may be safe."

Long before the rise of "totalitarian liberalism" the fathers of the American Constitution foresaw the danger. Long before Henry Adams they knew that "power is poison." They agreed with Blake:

> *The strongest poison ever known*
> *Came from Caesar's laurel crown.*

They anticipated Burckhardt: "Power is of its nature evil, whoever wields it. It is not a stability but a lust, and *ipso facto* insatiable, therefore unhappy in itself and doomed to make others unhappy." They even remembered that the law of nature, to which they constantly appealed, is not merely an excuse for claiming that God is on our side in every dispute, but a command to examine our consciences with anxious care.

Europe was ready to welcome such a polite and conservative revolution. Since the rise of the *philosophes* and the triumph of the Enlightenment in the drawing rooms of Paris, the despots had been growing benevolent. They agreed with Madison and James Wilson that governments should seek the happiness of society. Some of them, like Leopold of Tuscany, tried to compel their perplexed subjects to be happy.

But the despots learned, with Turgot, that it was not easy to use the royal prerogative, for the good of the people, at the cost of the privileges of the aristocracy. Thus the cautious, almost constitutional, revolution in the American colonies seemed to promise reform with the minimum of danger. The transatlantic news lent wings to the ambiguous words of Rousseau. And Lafayette gave the first two drafts of the "Declaration of the Rights of Man" to the American Minister in Paris, for comment and criticism. The Minister was Thomas Jefferson.

We need not here review the many reasons why the French Revolution was unlike the American — to the dismay of Burke, and of John Adams and Hamilton and Washington. The middle classes — who started both revolutions and who never lost control in the United States — desired liberty and feared the Hobbesian state. But the masses in France, who were poor in a fashion unknown to North America, desired equality. The partisans of equality are often glad to impose it by force, and are sometimes regretful of their handiwork — for the sword, while curing one abuse, tends to create another.

Long before the Battle of Waterloo Europe was agreed that revolution was not the road to Utopia, although it might be the road to hell. The terror, the blasphemies, and the military despotism discredited the words which had seemed harmless in American mouths. And along with the concept of revolution, the concept of "natural rights" was rejected. It now seemed little better than an invitation to anarchy.

In our own day the doctrine that communism must in time prevail throughout the world seems a plan for perpetual war. The early nineteenth century took the same view of the "inalienable rights of man." The French National Convention and the Emperor Napoleon had justified their wars of conquest by boasting that the mission of France was to impose these rights upon her backward neighbors. Not only were "rights" thereby discredited, but also the natural law from which they derived. And lamentably, in the course of freeing the Continent from Napoleon, nationalism was transformed into a semi-religious frenzy. The emerging democracy, with its enthusiasm and good will, was wedded to the sovereign state — the monster whose sole allegiance is to self-interest.

As early as 1802 Hegel ridiculed the philosophy of natural law. Within a few years he was preaching that the state is the one embodiment of moral value, that its "right" is the only right, that it is the manifestation of the Divine in history and the source of social value. (This is the same state from whose cold hands, for two thousand years, men had sought to save the things that are God's.) With the abandonment of the higher law, with the deification of selfish parochial sovereignty, with the mobilization behind that sinful faith of men's decent love for their homelands, the way was being cleared for the "total" wars of the twentieth century.

5

Ironically, the United States (whose freedom was founded on the law of nature) gave the best proof of how that law may be distorted when men identify "nature" with their own bad habits and forget that beyond nature lies God. Because the abolitionists called upon the higher law to discredit slavery, the slaveholders called upon it to defend their property in human bodies. Progress, they easily "proved," can only be made secure by slavery. Clearly it is the intention of "Nature and of Nature's God" that slavery should be the price of civilization.

"It is a great and dangerous error," wrote John Caldwell Calhoun, "to suppose that all people are equally entitled to liberty. It is a reward to be earned, not a blessing to be gratuitously lavished on all alike; — a reward reserved for the intelligent, the patriotic, the virtuous and deserving; — and not a boon to be bestowed on a people too ignorant, degraded and vicious, to be capable either of appreciating or enjoying it. . . . This dispensation seems to be the result of some fixed law."

We are back in the pre-Christian world — in Athens, which had 30,000 free citizens in a population of 500,000 and where no one dared imagine that the rights and benefits of the citizens could be extended to the stranger or to the slave. The Stoics were the first to proclaim, and the Christians the first to practice, the principle that the same law of nature must apply to all the children of God. And the post-Christian world quickly proved that when God is withdrawn from the picture (or is diluted into a Final Cause) the law of nature can excuse oppression as readily as it can defend justice.

Calhoun's gloss — and that of later jurists in the United States, for whom "nature" meant monopoly capitalism — explains the hostility of Holmes toward natural law, and toward "all talk of duties and rights." Such talk, in his experience, usually prefaced a decision that no man should be deprived of his right to work for fourteen hours a day, or for starvation wages. Yet the hopeful solution, as in the case of the polluted river, remains to purify rather than to abolish.

To combat the cynicism of those who would promote injustice in the name of a higher law, must we hand ourselves helpless to a bureaucracy that ignores the field in which government should not operate? "We shall triumph and we shall be Caesars," said Dostoyevsky's Grand Inquisitor, "and then we shall plan the universal happiness of man." If "law means force" and nothing else, how shall we escape the immense force of these persistent and impertinent Caesars who are so eager to plan our happiness?

At the moment we are not escaping. The Caesars are encroaching upon our lives each day more firmly — in part because we have sold our true defense in favor of what the nineteenth century called "historic rights."

The concept of historic rights is the Black Gospel of the sovereign state. It admits that man's rights are to be found in nature; but it identifies nature with the separate history of each small self-idolatrous group. The institutions of each state are the proper, the "natural," result of its history. They will alter with the passing centuries; but they will remain peculiar to each subdivision within society, characteristic of its unique autonomous history. They will never apply to mankind.

"I have seen Frenchmen, Italians, Russians," wrote Joseph de Maistre, "but as for Man, I declare I never met him in my life; if he exists, it is without my knowledge." If Maistre were still interested he might find Man today along those grim frontiers, built entirely upon graves, where "les Français, les Allemands et les Russes ne peuvent plus se battre que sur des tombes, tant elles sont pressées." He would not easily sort out the myriad bones into Frenchmen, Italians, Russians. They are Mankind, aspiring and betrayed, all subject to the same judgment and to the same God, all murdered by a false philosophy which denies both, but which asserts a puny local pride.

Instead of the rights of man, according to this philosophy, we have French rights, German rights, Russian rights — and perhaps Luxembourgian and Andorran rights. All these are real; but Man has become a fictional character.

The nineteenth century was obsessed with the origin and development of "national" institutions, "national" traits, "national" and exclusive interests. Historians gave their lives to showing why the nations had become what they were, why they had to be that way, why "shallow thinkers" in the Dark Ages had been misled into assuming a dream-unity for Christendom. The old, authentic European sense of a Great Society, the lingering nostalgic bequest of the Roman and the Holy Roman Empires, and of the once-universal Church, was called a "damnable heritage." Only a sentimentalist like Chesterton would retain the folly to write:

> *Dig for me where I fall, said he,*
> *Bear not my body home;*
> *For all the earth is Roman earth*
> *And I shall die in Rome.*

Modern man had outgrown such childishness. He knew there was nothing real except provincialism. Even the great Leopold von Ranke saw "universal history" as the history of national states, each at its own high moment contributing something distinctive, something forever German, forever Italian, but not under any circumstances European or Human. In the hand of a genius like Ranke this was a concept of dignity and worth, of distinction and self-respect; but when it was vulgarized by little men it became a concept of self-adulation for the elect. "The nation, which the age of Enlightenment hoped to see assimilated to mankind, is already, in Ranke's scheme, preparing to swallow the Human Race."

We may add that long before the Enlightenment the true sons of the West were struggling to prevent the nation, in Ranke's sense, from coming into being. The country, the language, the common history, the people who form a community within the larger whole: all this has been honored from the beginning. But the nineteenth-century nation, the pagan state which denies the Great Society, denies the common faith which is even holier than the parish loyalty: this is the new thing in our ancient West. This is the harbinger of the twentieth-century slaughter.

6

If the rights of man were the religion of the eighteenth-century *philosophes*, nationalism was the religion of the nine-teenth-century historian and journalist. The mystical father-land, with severely practical "interests," gathering all political and economic power into its hands, absorbing step by step the private and voluntary institutions of society which foster freedom, was made the new shrine for reverence and obedi-ence. Fénelon in the early eighteenth century could still pro-claim that patriotism did not absolve the citizen from his duties to mankind, and that no war is just except in the defense of freedom. This was not the French consensus in the days of Napoleon — or if it was, the words had become meaningless. When the national state has roused the popular passion all wars become wars against aggression. Patriotism, divorced from the cosmopolitan sense of a larger community, becomes "pooled self-esteem." And the members of the pool are con-fident that they can do no wrong.

The West is gravely menaced by such self-esteem. Our parochial sense of righteousness has been so inflated by the debasement of patriotism that we no longer seek the causes of war in human nature, in the partial corruption of all men's hearts. Since the members of our own little pool of pride are by definition "good," and since wars continue to afflict us, they must be caused by the members of some other pool, who are by definition "bad." Thus wars become steadily more "just" and more ferocious: the greater the war, the greater the self-esteem on both sides. Total wars, fought to the bit-

ter end of total surrender, are the maniacal creed of an inflamed democracy. "A war fought to the finish" is what the
democrats of Athens demanded in 431 B.C., when they drove
their city to its ruin. "A war fought to the finish" was the
joint demand of the United States and Great Britain at Casa-
blanca.

When war threatens, or is in progress, the modern nationalist politician dare not suggest that his own people may be
in part to blame. He dare not admit the perverted charm
of war, which is "at once a rest from responsibility and a
change from the tedium of civilized life. . . . The rattle and
frustration of highly organized industrial life sharpens and
shortens tempers; the boredom and monotony of that same
life lower our resistance to any course of action which seems
to offer excitement and opportunity." If we rule out such
reflections upon the wickedness in all our hearts, labeling
them unpatriotic, what can we do when the fighting impends
except assume an absolute virtue and impute an absolute vice?
And in such a case, what can be more reasonable than total
war?

An unflattering contrast, which reflects the mind of the
West before it succumbed to modern nationalism, is found in
Gibbon's famous chapter, "General Observations":

A philosopher may be permitted to enlarge his views, and
to consider Europe as one great republic, whose various
inhabitants have attained almost the same level of politeness
and cultivation. The balance of power will continue to
fluctuate, and the prosperity of our own, or the neighboring kingdoms, may be alternately exalted or depressed; but

these partial events cannot essentially injure our general state of happiness.

Gibbon then numbers the nations of Europe, adding that the divisions within the "great republic" are harmless, because "in peace, the progress of knowledge and industry is accelerated by the emulation of so many active rivals: in war, European forces are exercised by temperate and undecisive contests." The thought that one European state could plan the annihilation of another was inadmissible to Gibbon's mind. He lived in the days between the savage wars of religion and the savage wars of nationalism, when "temperate and undecisive contests" were the sign of civilization. He lived when the blackness as well as the grandeur of the human soul was common knowledge, when it was possible for all men to assume a share of blame for the calamities of history, when it was difficult for statesmen to feel that the whole of one nation was right and the whole of another nation wrong, when the old unity of the West had not been forgotten, and long before the suicide of the West had begun.

We cannot revive the eighteenth century, and we should doubtless be disappointed if we could. But may we not revive the fairest feature of that age: its lingering sense of the "one great republic"? Some of the downward steps from that high vision to our present poverty are clear. The progress of science and the rebirth of limited warfare bred a sense of security, of complacency, which survived the French Revolution and the Napoleonic wars and which flowered in that optimistic view of human nature and of progress which misled the nineteenth century. The undue optimism (especially when

God had faded into a vague Spirit of good will, a Celestial Social Worker) made the faith which stressed the depravity as well as the redemption of man seem outmoded, almost barbarous. Warnings against the deadliness of nationalism were ignored. Suggestions that science, which had begun to make mass-leisure possible, could just as easily provide mass-murder, were met by the oldest and silliest of arguments: that the frightfulness of the new weapons would cause us to abandon war.*

Security, complacency, optimism — they all seem old-fashioned today. But if we do not wish to replace them with anxiety and despair we must outgrow one more fetish of the nineteenth century: the sovereignty that is superior to natural law, incompatible with Western unity.

7

When we push reason and religion out of the door they sometimes return by the window. Having laughed at the higher law and at our obligations to the West, we now show a dawning sense of duty toward nature herself. This too is one of the oldest elements in our tradition, finding superb expression in the works of Virgil.

---

* In 1715 an Englishman encouraged himself as follows, on the subject of firearms: "Perhaps Heaven hath in Judgment inflicted the Cruelty of this invention, on purpose to fright Men into Amity and Peace, and into an Abhorrence of the Tumult and Inhumanity of War."

When Dante chose the Roman poet as his guide through Hell and Purgatory, he had in mind this natural piety. Virgil taught the dignity of labor to a society wherein slavery demeaned most manual work. The care for the soil, he said, and its preservation unwounded by man's greed, was essential not only materially but spiritually. To a proud pagan world he preached humility before the mystery of life. He sought to show that history is not mechanical, that it is filled with divine meaning — therefore must man protect his heritage and never squander it. Fortunately for our own proud pagan world, such thoughts are being reborn today in many minds.*

"Industrialism," writes Aldous Huxley, "is the systematic exploitation of wasting assets. In all too many cases, the thing we call progress is merely an acceleration in the rate of that exploitation. . . . As population goes up, the fertility of the ever more ruthlessly exploited land goes down. There is spreading and deepening human poverty in the midst of spreading and deepening natural poverty." These reflections lead Mr. Huxley to an attack on nationalism: "In actual fact we worship, not one God, but fifty or sixty little godlets, each of whom is, by definition, the enemy, actual or potential, of all the rest. . . . No individual can do his nationalistic duty without inflicting harm on some at least of his fellow men."

Michael Roberts agrees. He reminds us that "modern civilization is based on the consumption of irreplaceable natural resources," that modern man is at war with nature and there-

---

* The anticipations of the Christian world in Virgil are discussed in a book by Theodor Haecker, published in English under the title of *Vergil the Father of the West*.

fore with himself, and that unless he can learn once more to live within his earth-income "there will be sufferings and upheavals beside which the competition of rival empires and the squabbles of capitalist and factory-hand will appear to be the innocent amusements of children at play." Roberts implores us to understand in time that we have strictly limited reserves and that the possibilities of science are finite. And he concludes sorrowfully that so far as one can tell today "the world has enough oil to last for twenty-two years, enough coal to last five hundred, and enough damsilliness to last forever."

A new literature of exhortation has come into being, begging us to take note of the crimes we are committing against our planet. We are warned that the world supported three times as many people in 1950 as it did in 1750, and that during the same two centuries man has developed the tools for consuming with lunatic speed the assets of the earth — and especially that thin layer of soil which is our most precious and most rapidly dwindling possession. We are told that in the past thirty years we have lost more good soil than in the whole of previous history; and we are reminded, not without malice, that a Sunday newspaper in New York City consumes twenty acres of timber for a single issue.

Men who would deny that a natural law governs their treatment of their neighbors are beginning to admit that they have no "right" to abuse grass or trees. Men who would support a national policy which condemns friendly nations to poverty and unemployment, tell us that we must not condemn the bison to extinction. It is our duty, they say, to treat nature with piety and charity and forebearance. They quote Greek texts to show that such is the ancient wisdom. Frequently they miss the texts which apply the same wisdom to mankind.

Yet this is most hopeful. If the movement spreads it may save our society. A proper piety toward birds may lead us into a proper piety toward Belgians. The same law governs our relations to both: we must not give back a broken and brutalized world, at the end of our tenure. We are brief trustees. If we are too lazy or incompetent to improve the trust, we should at least refrain from wasting it at a casino.

"The end of man is to create science," wrote the Spanish philosopher, Unamuno, "to catalogue the universe, so that it may be handed back to God in order." And Georges Bernanos writes: "Inch by inch we shall regain the universe which we have lost through sin, and we shall return it to You as we received it on the first morning of the world, orderly and holy."

The Spaniard and the Frenchman find a motive for natural piety in serving God and respecting His universe. The recent literature of conservation does not examine motives. It assumes — which is most interesting — that any sane man will be shocked at the thought of destroying what he cannot replace, impoverishing the far future, turning good land into desert, or abolishing an entire species of beasts. But why should he be shocked? What difference does it make, if there is no law but man's puny force, no truth, no rights or duties beyond the conventions of the community? The world will last *us* out, in any case, and will last our children for several generations. Why bother about a few more Gobi deserts or a few less varieties of fowl? Surely we touch something very deep if we admit that such impiety is not right? For what can we mean by "right"?

We asked in the Introduction: "Can there be any sanction for good conduct if the will of God is excluded as unknowable or non-existent?" And we admitted that the notion of God is disquieting to many of our neighbors. Yet it keeps recurring, whenever men behave with disinterest. The thought of handing back the world to God in good order, as we first received it, gives dignity to what else might be "a long fool's errand to the grave." The thought of worrying about what happens to Pittsburgh in five hundred years, when the coal runs out, is neither dignified nor sane.

At the risk of offense, we wonder whether the men and women who are worrying so eloquently and so effectively today may not be moved by emotions more profound than they admit. When they woke from the dream of "progress" to find modern man violating the earth that nourished him, did they not feel with Bernanos, "ce n'est pas votre maison . . . c'est la maison commune, bénie par le Christ"?

Even the cleverest thinkers, when they insist on secular reasons for man's occasional bursts of good conduct, seem to talk nonsense. David Hume, for example, who pleased himself with the thought that he had refuted natural law, wrote as follows: "Having found that natural as well as civil justice derives its origins from human conventions, we shall quickly perceive how fruitless it is to resolve the one into the other, and seek in the laws of nature a stronger foundation for our political duties than interest and human conventions, while these laws themselves are built on the very same foundation."

Will "interest and human conventions" lead us to deal piously with nature, mercifully with man? Will they give us the strength of Antigone to resist the trespassing state? Will they encourage us to build a brotherly community in our half-ravished, half-frightened West?

Those who walked such paths in the past thought they were following a higher law. Perhaps we can regain that faith if we practice the newly-recommended reverence toward nature. If we behave like men who believe in the law we may surprise ourselves one day by finding it is true. Man, says Unamuno, does not become good by believing in God; he comes to believe in God by being good.

Chapter Six

✫　　✫　　✫　　✫　　✫

" A Sufficient Moral Unanimity? "

Chapter Six

The question now is whether the peoples of the countries which are still free are capable of attaining, by the paths of liberty and of the spirit, a sufficient moral unanimity.

JACQUES MARITAIN

W E HAVE SAID that Western man lives in two societies, with divided loyalties, because he has discovered and rediscovered the life-giving distinction between Church and state. He has insisted upon an area of freedom for his own spirit. So long as that dualism survives, Western man may be said to live four lives which overlap but which are sharply separate. He lives in the family as a husband and father, in the Church as a soul seeking salvation, in the world of business as a breadwinner, and in the world of politics as a citizen with duties toward the government that serves him — but does not own him. And if he values this fourfold life he must remember that the most harmless, constitution-bound government is forever tempted toward absolutism, toward becoming a "state" instead of a public utility.

Politicians are rightly ambitious and citizens are naturally lazy. No sooner has a government been put into its proper place than it begins to swell once more. The very men who had diminished it, or their children, applaud the perilous growth — because they find no easier defense from civil strife, or religious hatreds, or economic chaos.

The challenge and the danger of Western life is here exposed. Continually we face the unanswerable question: How far dare we use government without risking loss of control, without evoking that satanic monster, Leviathan? Our tentative replies must be reassessed with every change in the methods of production, every shift in the balance between population and resources. Yet two facts remain unchanging through the ages.

First, so long as we preserve the division between the things that are God's and the things that are Caesar's we may alter within wide limits the relations between the four parts of man's life: family, church, business, government. Indeed the structure of our society in any era will be revealed if we ask which parts are paramount. During the Middle Ages, for example, the feudal family was dominant over business and frequently ignored government; but the first power was the Church. In the seventeenth century government gained at the expense of the Church and undertook the detailed regulation of business; the family was diminished but still morally strong. In the latter nineteenth century — the days of the robber barons in America and the *ventres dorés* in France — business gained hugely at the expense of government; the Church waned and with it the family. Today government is again taking charge of business, while the Church and the family remain relatively frail. Thus we have feudalism, mercantilism, capitalism, and the welfare state — in terms of the four main ingredients of our lives. We shall never find the perfect balance between them, for the dangers and opportunities of this world change faster than our minds can follow.

Second, if we abandon our basic division, our dualism, the government will promptly become a "state" and will absorb all four ingredients. It will tell us what to think, thus denying the freedom of conscience and of religion. It will swallow the world of business, thus making us helpless before the bureaucrat. And it will then do what it chooses with the family. In Hitler's Germany and Stalin's Russia it chose to demand that all men become spies and informers upon their next of kin. At that stage the family perishes unless it can produce a large number of Antigones — which brings us back to Sophocles' "unwritten and undying laws of God."

This is not an argument for a Jeffersonian government, frugal and unassuming. It is an argument for ceaseless watchful care over the separation between Church and state. In the free world today most nations are deeply and sensibly concerned about the proper structure of society, the proper relation between the four parts of our lives. We should find a workable (though temporary) answer, if we do not relax our vigilance against Leviathan.

The safeguards (the constitutional forms) that we impose upon our governments must cause them to be clumsier and slower than the tyrant states. Why should we repine? This is merely another aspect of our everlasting problem: How can we make government powerful and efficient (so as to use it for defense and for social reform) without making it our master? It is the riddle of the Sphinx, "which not to answer is to be destroyed." It is also the burden of freedom. If we bear it wisely the West may come

> *To serve as model for the mighty world,*
> *And be the fair beginning of a time.*

2

Today we face three strong temptations to forget or to deny the riddle, and thus to lose our liberties and our souls. The first is fear — the Hobbesian fear which we discussed in Chapter One and which we have seen illustrated throughout history, the fear which drove Rome to murder Carthage and Corinth and her own character as well.

Ours is doubtless a perilous time; but we make it more so by our refusal to ask whether the enemy may also feel frightened, and whether his fears may also seem justified. Fear has often led nations into making themselves so "safe" that their neighbors felt desperate, and the result has often been a war which produced a worse predicament than the one from which it started.

Modern armaments are hedged in secrecy and fear. They exact a high toll upon the civil rights of the citizen. If there is to be no limit to our "safety" there can be no limit to the abandonment of our liberties. We may thus have lost the war for Western freedom before we begin it — which will not prevent us from feeling that we are "virtuous defenders of a great cause, beset by scoundrels," or from fighting to the ferocious end.

Fear leads to boasting, and boasting to an unworthy misprisal of the foe. Our leaders tell us that they wait eagerly for "real evidence of a change in Soviet intentions." But in view of their ever increasing self-praise what evidence are they likely to find convincing? And when they have made the West much stronger will they become much more humble? Or has the habit of loud language seized them?

Clearly, our duty is to grow strong; but can we not do so without hate? And can we not remember that we are weak because we were sated with self-slaughter at the end of our last war within the West? We threw away our arms. We decided that men had become trustful as a result of forty years of fighting and that the sword was outmoded. This was not Russia's doing. In fact, as Arnold Toynbee keeps reminding us, if Russia stops short of war she will have been a blessing in bear's clothing. She will have forced us to help each other — and even to be intermittently polite to each other — within our once-Christian world.

The Hobbesian fear, the fear of making the first charitable gesture, is immoral and therefore debasing. If we continue to indulge it we may reach such depths that we invent an enemy in order to explain our own state of nerves — as Rome invented the notion that broken Carthage might still ruin her.

And yet our governments encourage fear. They defend every generous design, every step toward Western unity, not on its merits but as a grim plan to frustrate the Kremlin. Have they decided that we are lost to greatness and can only be moved by fright? Let us remind them that it is not true. And let us remind ourselves that frightened men cannot be free. If we permit the spread of this contagion we shall find that while searching for "safety" we jettison the meaning of the West and land ourselves in a unitary state.

The appropriate reply to danger was given by Charles Péguy, who died fighting for France in 1914:

> When a free people is threatened with military invasion . . . it needs only to prepare perfectly its mobilization. And its mobilization once prepared, needs only to continue . . . its life of culture and liberty. Any change in this existence caused by the introduction of fear, of apprehension, or even of expectation, would already mean a successful attempt, a beginning of this military, barbarous and enslaving invasion . . . the most dangerous of invasions: the invasion which crosses the threshold of inner life and which is infinitely more dangerous for a people than a territorial occupation." *

Here is a freedom worth defending. But how far, today, do we protect "the threshold of inner life"? Péguy speaks for the West. If we cannot hear him the West is dying in our hearts.

3

Our second temptation is to deny the riddle by forgetting it exists, by forgetting that there must somewhere be a limit to what government can do. Thus we may overload our politi-

* Péguy continues: "Pareillement un simple citoyen, quand il a mis prête et quand il tient prête sa petite mobilisation individuelle, il n'a plus qu'à continuer de son mieux son petit train-train de vie d'honnête homme; car il n'y a rien de mieux au monde qu'une vie d'honnête homme; il n'y a rien de meilleur que le pain cuit des devoirs quotidiens."

cal systems, which are by nature inefficient so long as they remain free. If they break under the weight we shall be forced by our own excesses to call in the tyrant state.

The danger line is passed when the heads of executive departments can no longer keep track of their subordinates, or when the legislature can no longer keep track of the executive departments. Beyond that point responsible government ceases. Yet by the time the point is reached, business must be largely under political control. The vast powers cannot suddenly be abandoned, lest production cease. So new powers are assumed in order to "cure" the self-made chaos. A nation of honest patriots is transformed into an irresponsible "state."

Sooner or later every "state" must remake the citizen to suit the bureaucrat; for the perversity of free men's behavior and the variety of free men's souls would outwit a board of totalitarian "planners" which contained no member less imaginative than Shakespeare, less clearheaded than Aristotle.

Early in 1939 the Economic Adviser to the Bank of England wrote:

It is possible that the strain is not yet excessive, that the Ministers and Members we can expect to get to serve us, in addition to supervising adequately Defence, Order and Justice, Health, Education and Social Security, egalitarian taxation and the smoothing out of the trade cycle — with the financial policies incidental to all these — can find time, knowledge and energy in addition to regulate production, fix prices and wages, arrange markets for industry, and take charge of the moral and mental direction of the citizen's life; but I think it unlikely.

One day we may invent new forms of government which can attempt these tasks without becoming tyrants. But until we do — or until we invent a business system that does not need policing — let us remember the riddle of the Sphinx. Let us seek "planned" welfare for the West at any cost save that of our liberty.

> There is little doubt that competent, well-informed and unhurried planning can, in many fields, produce better results than haphazard competition, but the cost is far higher than people have yet realized and the penalties for incompetence far more severe: in place of individual bankruptcies and large-scale unemployment one has the possible breakdown of a whole country.

Government can serve, can help; but if it takes full charge it must enslave us.

4

Our third temptation is to deny or forget the riddle in the name of nationalism. This is a new poison for which we must find a new drug.

We have seen that the modern nations emerged from the ruins of the Holy Roman Empire and the schisms within the Church. Patriotism in the Middle Ages had centered upon a province or a city, or upon Christendom, rather than upon a nation. Even in England, which first developed a true sense of national unity, the government ruled Irishmen, Welshmen, Englishmen, and Frenchmen — and for long the official language was French.

The eighteenth century, although nationalism was widely preached, remained international, cosmopolitan: the *philosophes* boasted that they were "citizens of the world" devoted to the good of "humanity." They saw the nations as convenient units for promoting this good. They saw Europe as essentially "one great republic." The "enlightened" man, they taught, should first rid his own nation of abuses and superstitions, and should then help his neighbors to do likewise. The result would be peace and progress.

The change began with the French Revolution. The "Declaration of the Rights of Man" said that "the principle of all sovereignty resides essentially in the nation. No body or individual may exercise any authority which does not proceed directly from the nation." The statement sounds so commonplace that most men today would take it for granted. Yet the statement, as we have tried to show, is incompatible with the West.

Marie Joseph Chénier said to the Convention: " . . . on the ruins of the dethroned superstitions can be founded the one natural religion, having neither sects nor mysteries. Her preachers are our legislators, her priests our executive officers of the state. In the temple of this religion humanity will offer incense only on the altar of our country, the mother of us all and our divinity."

The use of religious language was justified, for this hate-breeding nationalism — the worship of "our" country and "our" divinity, superior to all others — has been the religion of millions in the modern world. It has its rituals, its dogmas, its persecutions. Among its barbarized victims the will of the nation is the will of God. "One dare not hope," said the implacable Saint-Just to the Convention, "that things will improve so long as one foe of Freedom breathes. . . . After the French people has announced its will everything which is contrary to its will stands outside the sovereignty of the nation; and who stands outside the sovereign is his enemy."

What is the choice between this profane theory of sovereignty as "the will of the French people" and National Socialism as explained in the *Beamtenkalender* of 1937:

> Since there is, in the national socialist state, no difference, let alone opposition, between the state as a separate legal structure and the totality of citizens . . . since the state consists here of the totality of citizens, united in a common destiny by common blood and a common philosophy of life and comprised in a single organization, it is neither necessary nor possible to define a sphere of freedom for the individual citizen as against the state.

Yet that "sphere of freedom" is the meaning and the strength of the West: that area, first cleared during the Middle Ages, where the state may not enter, where man is left to seek his own salvation and thus to grow into a responsible human person. Any theory of absolute sovereignty, whether wrapped in the language of freedom or of Germanic power worship, is the mortal enemy of the West. The liberty to seek the truth and to serve it, which has given us our saints and our scientific objectivity, is the *élan* of our society. Our vast vitality, our richness of personality, all stem from this. Yet the new nationalism "daily devours apace, and nothing said."

Unhappily the French Revolution was democratic as well as nationalistic. Thus two great forces of the modern world, which might have grown separately, were born twins. When France made war on Austria in 1792 she fought to impose democracy. The Convention declared that

> the French nation . . . will treat as enemies every people who, refusing liberty and equality or renouncing them, may wish to maintain, recall, or treat with the prince and the privileged classes . . . it engages not to subscribe to any treaty and not to lay down its arms . . . until the people shall have adopted the principles of equality and founded a free and democratic government.

This is harsh language. Liberty and equality, freedom and democracy, have been transformed from humanitarian hopes into totalitarian commands. Sixteen years earlier, in the American Declaration of Independence, these were the "rights of man" for which it was permissible to strive. Suddenly they become orders from the General. Anyone who is a day late in becoming "equal" will be shot. And so will anyone who argues. We have moved from Thomas Jefferson to the Committee on Un-American Activities, from the law of conscience to the law of Senator McCarthy.*

---

* The Senator, to be sure, does not kill those that resist his brand of "Americanism." He prefers to defame them gradually, and safely.

A new flag, a new song, new shrines, new ceremonies, new clothes — a new conscript army, a new journalism and a new system of education under which the children belonged to the nation and not to the parents — all helped to tie the new democracy to the poisonous pagan worship of the state. "Children belong to the Republic," said Barère. "The Republic leaves to parents the guidance of your first years, but as soon as your intelligence forms itself the Republic proudly claims the rights it holds over you. You are born for the Republic." The statement would not have surprised Scipio Africanus, or Philip of Macedonia, or the Emperor Diocletian, or Adolph Hitler; but it would have surprised most citizens of the West from Gregory the Great to Edward Gibbon.

Commenting on Barère, Carlton Hayes writes:

> "The People" has become "the nation," a mystical entity, an absolute sovereign, a Moloch not only of classes but of individuals. It catechizes its own citizens, and by force it seeks to catechize the citizens of other nations. It conscripts youth for war or for schools and abrogates the historic rights of the father and the family. It can seize everything and destroy everything, for above it there is no law. . . . It has a horror of divisions, schisms, minorities. It labors for unity, uniformity, concentration. . . . Its vaunted liberty, in last analysis, is not for the individual but for the national state. The nation may do whatever it will, the individual may do only what the national state determines.

Georges Bernanos imagines a dialogue between the State, which is our enemy, and the Fatherland, which is the source and center of our patriotism. Paraphrasing and slightly parodying a speech by Barère before the Convention, the State pleads supreme danger and demands "that the civic liberties of every citizen between the ages of eighteen and fifty should be suppressed and that these men should be constrained blindly to obey the leaders I have appointed."

The Fatherland answers:

> The mere idea of such an exaction is cruel and sacrilegious, and I forbid you to ask anything of the sort in my name. . . . The measure you are asking me to approve would open a huge breach in the walls of the Christian City. Through it my liberties will vanish one by one, for they are all dependent on each other, like the beads of the Rosary. . . . The very name of Fatherland will be wiped from the minds of men. For the Fatherlands belong to the Order of Christ's Charity . . . and who would dare to recognize them in these maddened brutes, fighting like ravening bitches for the carcass of the world?

There speaks the patriot as opposed to the nationalist. Loving his own country, the patriot respects the virtues of other people and other lands. He rejoices in the variety of the world and in a sense of brotherhood. But the nationalist is only at home among the fellow members of his "pool of self-esteem." The patriot can die for his country in charity; but the nationalist cannot even live without hating.

The contrast was movingly expressed by H. G. Wells in 1929. "I loathe nationalism," he wrote, "but this does not prevent my being intensely, affectionately, and profoundly English. . . . I am a scion, however unworthy, of a very great race, and heir to an unapproachable tradition of candid speech and generous act." And he added that the English are a people "necessary to mankind." * All the great peoples are necessary to mankind. And it is necessary that they remain intensely themselves, widely different from other peoples, lest mankind perish of boredom and standardization. But it is not necessary that each government serving such peoples should interpret their "interests" with the selfishness of a panther guarding its kill.

The walls of Bernanos' Christian City were breached by the French Revolution as early as 1792, when religion was "secularized" and the state took over all education, social welfare, and charity. The people must be taught that their religion was the Republic, and that it brought no gospel of peace. The war which France began against Austria continued with one short interruption for twenty-five years. It was the first war in which democratic and national passions combined, and before it was over it involved not only France and Austria, but Italy, England, Spain, the Germanies, Russia, and the United States. (The latter country, surprisingly, found time to fight on both sides.)

During this long agony the foes of France cultivated their own aggressive nationalisms, while slowly the sense of Euro-

---

* "All men are by nature partisans and patriots," Wells had written some years before, "but the natural tribalism of men in the nineteenth century was unnaturally exaggerated, it was fretted and overstimulated and inflamed and forced into the nationalist mould. Nationalism was taught in schools, emphasized by newspapers, preached and mocked and sung into men. Men were brought to feel they were as improper without a nationality as without their clothes in a crowded assembly. Oriental peoples who had never heard of nationality before, took to it as they took to the cigarettes and bowler hats of the West."

pean unity expired.* Yet as late as the mid-nineteenth century most Western nations were not strictly national states. Neither Germany nor Italy was united, and the empires of Austria, Russia, and Turkey included many peoples. In the United States the Civil War had not yet insured that the central government should alone be sovereign. Before the end of the century, however, three influences had combined to exacerbate the selfish aspects of sovereignty, and thus to complete the work which the French Revolution had begun.

The first was a revived militarism, engendered in large part by the wars for national unification. The second was the spread of the industrial revolution — a neutral factor, which many good men hoped would lend itself to internationalism, but which was used instead to promote the new superstition. The Industrial Revolution broke down local self-sufficiency and autonomy, provided the communication systems which are essential to a large centralized bureaucratic state, and made available the funds and equipment for universal free schooling, modern journalism, and modern propaganda. These innovations might all have served the cause of Western unity; but they were appropriated to spread the poison of nationalist history, parochial pride, international mistrust.

The third influence toward dividing and embittering the West was economic nationalism, which was revived in the United States in the eighteen-sixties, and on the Continent a little later. The high priest was Friedrich List, a German

---

* England never became fanatical in the new faith, as did Germany and other conquered countries; but England had possessed a healthy sense of patriotism and unity in the days when the French were still primarily Burgundians, Provençals, Normans, Gascons.

who moved to America. List agreed with Fichte and Hegel that the nation-state was the only important unit. Neither the individual, nor the West, nor "humanity," counted against the interest of the state. And since no two states were ever in precisely the same stage of industrialization, each should "protect" itself against the products of its more advanced or more backward neighbors. Trade, which the liberals had hoped might unite the world, became one more excuse for the disintegration of society. List died in 1846; but the German tariff of 1879 was his monument.

Let us review the dangers of this third temptation to deny the riddle and sell the West to monism: by the end of the nineteenth century love of country was being unusually degraded into contempt for foreigners; national "interest" was being as usual exalted above the moral law; the lingering slight sense of a Western community was being termed "sentimental"; and the new benighted national schools were teaching a form of self-centered history that would have made Gibbon wince. The way was being cleared for the great wars.

We have survived two such calamities, with our dualism impaired but not destroyed, impaired but not irreparable. The Hegelian-Marxist state, wherein the private conscience is nationalized, has not yet dragged down the West from within or from without. And the "totalitarian liberals" have not yet enslaved us to paternalism. But could we survive a third war, a third "victory"? If anybody was left alive who remembered Western values, and if the devastation was so great that a centralized bureaucracy became impossible (so that the timid could not take refuge in tyranny), the West might be revived: a little dizzy, a little radioactive, but still willing to let each man save or lose his own soul.

On the other hand, if we would stop impoverishing each other in the name of our "national interests," there should be no need for a third victory. If we practiced our own great faith, who would dare attack us?

5

What can we do about these dangers to our society: fear, big government, and the new nationalism? Since they threaten the moral basis of life we must seek moral defenses.

The problem of big government is largely a problem of slackness. We yield at every temptation to shift the burden of responsibility, to ask too much of politics, too little of ourselves. And indeed if our sole standard is physical well-being how shall we resist the impulse to meet each crisis by passing a few more laws, or by ordering a few more scores of aircraft? Thus we shall feel increasingly aggrieved, as we wait for the prosperity and safety that never come.

Moral inertia is to blame, for it inspires us to cling pathetically to the outworn faith in mechanical progress. Yet we have been shown in a hard school that every advance in knowledge is as likely to be used for evil as for good, and that progress is not a problem of physics but of the will.

The findings of science are a neutral force. They can as

easily lead us to death as to prosperity — more easily if prosperity is our only conscious aim. The greater the neutral force at our disposal, the more desperate becomes our need for a high purpose.

The scientific point of view, the objective measure of truth applied to the facts, is one of the glories of the Western spirit. And many men of science have been counted among our noblest citizens. But the practical results of their work are neither glorious nor shameful, neither noble nor wicked, until we have decided how to use them.

Yet as Professor John Baillie writes, "what is left for modern man to believe in, if he can no longer believe that the future is likely to be better than the past, or that his children's children are likely to inhabit a world less full of wrong than he himself has had to live in?"

Two points of view are left, after the wreck of the naïve progress-myth — and they are contending for the soul of the West today. One is the doctrine of the revolution, which admits that progress will not come of itself, merely through the widening of knowledge in a free society, but which insists that it can be imposed from above by the ruthless makers of five-year plans. "We shall be Caesars and then we shall plan the universal happiness of man" — the perfect state, delivered at once, maintained indefinitely by force and by the murder of those who do not appreciate its perfections. If we doubt that our deepest human needs can thus be met, or our most tragic sorrows alleviated, we have but one recourse: we must transfer progress into its proper field and make our aim the fulfillment of our moral natures.

The phrase may be taken in a Christian or a secular sense. In either case it means that we seek such virtues as disinterestedness, magnanimity, self-sacrifice, humility, love. There is no conflict between the Christian and the non-Christian as to the supremacy of these virtues: yet it has come to seem eccentric to suggest putting them first.

These are political as well as moral values, related to the most practical facts of life. The smallest progress in serving them might save the West from a revolution of terror and materialism. A little disinterestedness could transform our society, weakening the divisions between nations and between classes. And without humility we find ourselves treating our foes as devils, thus denying the sacredness of human personality as arrogantly as any commissar. How shall we win the hesitating millions, without humility? And let us remember that President Abraham Lincoln agreed with our Lord that "all the law and the prophets" were in His two commandments concerning love. Lincoln confessed it ruefully, a few months before the end of the Civil War, when he had just failed to find support in his Cabinet for a plan to pay the South (which was already clearly beaten) $400,000,000 for the emancipated slaves, so that there might be no bitterness, and an end to the killing. "The Rebels would misconstrue it," said the Secretary of the Navy. Yet it was superb politics, which would have averted decades of hatred, and for the South decades of poverty and despair.

If a President of the United States could recommend such plans, is it silly to suggest a slight increase in virtue for the salvation of our society? Is not this the reason we love freedom — that only a free man can attempt self-improvement? And do we not dread a totally planned society (aside from the fact that any sensible "planner" would doubtless execute us) because in field after field of human activity, plan by plan, the practice of virtue (or of vice) is made impossible? The state can have no virtue aside from that of its members. And in the end the only virtue left for the miserable members is obedience, the only vice is the richness of human personality that has long been the boast of the West.

Such reflections might arm us to deny our governments that last fatal extension of economic control which takes them beyond the point of no return; for thereafter they must either demoralize us into silent submission, or else allow production to collapse for the lack of a dictator's powers. On these grounds we can stand and say "No." But if welfare is our one purpose, how shall we ever halt the tide of laws, programs, plans and restrictions, before we have accepted so many rules that they can only be administered by a Stalin?

On the other hand, if we merely say "No" in the face of remediable hardship we shall be beaten by the men who preach that freedom is an excuse for selfishness, that no one but a tyrant can supply a sufficient standard of living, and that the soul is in any case nonsense.

Surely this need not be a serious dilemma? We are not suggesting an other-wordly personal salvation as a release from our neighborly duties. While denying that the regimented, dictated life can bring happiness, we are asserting that for Christian and non-Christian alike fulfillment means generosity here on earth. Although we do not hope for perfection, we emphatically hope for progress. But we insist that progress, even in the mundane form of social security, must follow upon the service of that eternal law which teaches that all men have equal moral dignity and thus equal basic rights.

The alternative to solving a problem by means of government is not to deny that the problem exists. And the refusal to accept too much government does not deny that over vast areas of modern life government may be the guardian of justice.

The price of freedom is the acceptance of responsibility. Since the dawn of the Middle Ages this has been the creed of the West. It is what Michael Roberts meant when he wrote, on the eve of the Second World War: "a religious conviction of the reality of right and wrong is . . . the only practical alternative to the deification of the state. . . . An outlook which absolves the individual from any need for responsibility and humility, and offers flattering and consoling doctrines in place of stubborn fact, is itself one of the chief causes of the disillusion and loss of moral tension which Spengler and the fascists mistook for biological degeneration."

The West has proved abundantly, since those days, that it is not biologically degenerate. We can still produce the requisite force and impudence to rock the planet. Before long we can doubtless abolish the moon if she displeases us, and make war on Mars if the American Senate fears his faintly red glow. But although the Spenglerian diagnosis was mistaken, the "disillusion and loss of moral tension" remain true, and need explaining. Are they not chargeable to the fact that it has become unfashionable to seek the remedy for social wrongs in moral imperatives? Legislation is no proper substitute for conscience.

6

This is not a counsel of despair, or a belated discovery that the problems of the world would be simplified if men were good. For when we consider the other dangers to our dualism (fear, and the aggressive, selfish, new nationalism) we shall find a pressing specific task which we must accomplish if we are to survive — a task which is consonant with the whole of our history and which does not require us to become good, but only slightly better.

More than a hundred years ago Franz Grillparzer coined the aphorism: "From humanity through nationality to bestiality." It is fitting that an Austrian poet should have put the case so cogently when nationalism was still adolescent; for Austria was heir to the Holy Roman Empire, to a decadent but living sense of European unity. She was striving (vainly and stupidly, but nevertheless striving) to build a large and loosely-knit society with many peoples and languages and ways of life. Austria gave Lord Acton hope that we might escape from nationalism, of which he wrote in 1862: "Its course will be marked with material as well as moral ruin, in order that a new invention may prevail over the works of God and the interests of mankind. There is no principle of change, no phase of political speculation conceivable, more comprehensive, more subversive, or more arbitrary than this."

Acton believed that the presence of many peoples under a unifying but limited authority would have the same effect as the separation of church from state, or as the separation of powers under the American Constitution. "It provides," he wrote, "against the servility which flourishes under a single authority, by balancing interests, multiplying associations. ... Liberty provokes diversity and diversity preserves liberty. ... The co-existence of several nations under the same state is ... one of the chief instruments of civilization; and, as such, it is in the natural and providential order, and indicates a state of greater advancement than the national unity which is the ideal of modern liberalism."

Today the praise of balanced powers is a commonplace to free men — but we apply the concept only to our tight little national boxes. Because we rejected the "state of greater advancement" we now find ourselves a prey to fear and in danger of self-extinction — like Hellas of old.

The fear may take grotesque forms, as in the American senators who insult the freedom of conscience by demanding that men bare their private opinions or else go to jail because they "might" be dangerous. It may take subtler forms, as in the case of Englishmen and Frenchmen who preach "neutralism" because America "might" heedlessly let slip the atom bomb: "No annihilation without representation." *

The fear is pervading. It poisons the lower levels of poli-

* Arnold Toynbee, who invented the phrase, preaches Atlantic Union; but most of the people who quote him are afraid even of uniting with their friends.

tical discussion and makes much of our popular journalism resemble the catcalls of ragamuffins. More importantly, it deprives the West of dignity at a time when we would woo the souls of our neighbors. We tell them we stand for freedom, and they ask what freedom have the people whom the senators pillory? We mumble about our Christian past, and they ask whether Christianity teaches men to despise and abuse their enemies? Fear is an unbecoming affliction, allied to boasting, whereas confidence is allied to humility.

And why are we afraid? Presumably because we feel weak. And why do we feel weak? Partly because we chose disarmament, and partly because our trade routes, our money markets, and our national borders are tightly closed like a fist.* "Our" wage scales, "our" full employment, "our" little plans and restrictions — each nation feels them sacred and will discuss relaxing them only if the project can be clothed in the unseemly garb of "enlightened self-interest." We never mention the grandeur of building a City of Man among the hundreds of millions who share an ancient faith.

We all believe in freedom of conscience and the sanctity of the individual — Christians and Jews and anticlericals and atheists alike. We all believe there is a law of right conduct, written in our hearts, which no government can repeal. Most of us believe it is our duty to deal gently, carefully, with our Father's house of which we are brief custodians. We even dare to boast these beliefs across the air-waves, before a

* The United States, for obvious reasons, would welcome a multilateral opening of the first two fists; but she is grieved if anyone even mentions the third.

skeptical mankind, and in the name of our Western community. But we have not dared create that community.

Instead we make ready to hurl mountains at our foes in the next war, scarring the universe like Lucifer and his lost angels. We narrow each day the area in which our citizens are permitted their own thoughts, their own discoveries or mistakes. We help our friends with one hand in the name of "defense," and savage them with the other in the name of "national interest." Because the United States is the strongest unit in the West, and is forced at times to make decisions out of her strength, her friends fear her even while praising her — yet they do not press for a Western community on Lord Acton's lines, wherein limited and balanced powers would prevent the strong from overbearing the weak, wherein patriotism and the variety of our culture would flourish, and only the dog in the manger would feel oppressed.

Fear and selfish nationalism — nationalism and more economic controls — economic controls and more big government — big government and more nationalism, more fear — we are trapped in an ugly cage of our own contriving, and we shall not escape by asking politicians please to save us. "Poor men that we are," wrote Madariaga in 1928, "we crawl dejected amidst national Gods . . . exposed to their awful whims and passions. . . . And thus are we progressing along a freely chosen path which leads to slavery."

Even when self-interest and fear drive us to seek an escape from the cage, all we can contrive under the old rules is the North Atlantic Treaty Organization — one more effort at co-operation which is half smothered in nationalism. We must not blame the politicians. No one can change the old rules but us, the Western people. And we shall not find the bold will to change them from fear, or from poverty, or from threats of communism, but only from virtue and the genius of the West. The answer is in our souls, very nearly in our bones; but we still ignore it in the service of Moloch, whom we took to be God, and who ordered us to divide our community into small self-idolatrous chunks.

> *Moloch . . . the strongest and the fiercest spirit*
> *That fought in Heaven . . .*
> *His trust was with the Eternal to be deem'd*
> *Equal in strength, and rather than be less*
> *Cared not to be at all.*

This is the very spirit of the God-state that we have lately obeyed: "armed with Hell-flames and fury all at once." We have not only bowed to Moloch but we have taught all the innocent East to worship him; for who ever heard of nationalism east of Suez until we made men "feel they were as improper without a nationality as without their clothes?"

Belatedly, we now seek to reassemble the severed pieces of our West — but only for defense, only in a league to meet the dangers which we acknowledge today. Yet the dangers change bewilderingly. One dictator burns like a torch in the midst of his dying town, only that another dictator may arise. Allied to the gallant Chinese we incinerate hundreds of thousands of treacherous Japs, only to ally ourselves with the gallant Japanese against the treacherous Chinamen. And some of the best friends of the United States forgot to change "gallant" into "treacherous" fast enough to gratify the Senate. And some of the best enemies of Hitler would revive him from his petrol pyre — blood-saturated followers and all — because our lately-gallant ally, Marshal Stalin, now displeases them.

Since we do not know who will be gallant and treacherous next, or for how long, no treaties or leagues will suffice. In a time of "spreading and deepening human poverty in the midst of spreading and deepening natural poverty" we shall meet with many sharp surprises. The human race is at war with nature and therefore with itself. If we are to help we must put our own house in order — the house where men believe in the higher law and the inner freedom and the pursuit of a truth that is absolute. We may then start to become strong and disinterested and humble, instead of weak and suspicious and braggart.

The West can be no help to mankind until she is indeed the West, and not a congeries of self-seeking tribes. Such tribes in brief alliance can win (or lose) a cold war. But a united West might give the wide world a chance for renewal.

In September 1951 Mr. Lester Pearson, the Foreign Minister of Canada, proclaimed that "the North Atlantic Treaty is more than a mere military alliance. . . . It is the nucleus of a future North Atlantic Community of free nations. . . . If a North Atlantic Federation is ever to develop now is the time when the solid foundations must be laid." Now is the time, in other words, when we the people must give a strong backing of faith and emotion to leaders who seek an escape from the Moloch state.

We could make a good case for Mr. Pearson in the light of geopolitics; for Sir Harold Mackinder's nightmare (or Hitler's dream) has at last come true: a single power controls the center of the land mass of the world, the great plain that runs from eastern Germany to Siberia and from the Baltic to the Black Sea. "Who rules the heartland commands the world-island" (the European-Asiatic continent), wrote Mackinder, and "who rules the world-island commands the world." Since we do not intend to be commanded by the present rulers we are wrenching the globe on its axis and making the Atlantic Ocean rather than the Eurasian plain the center of world power. But from Germany to the Pacific Ocean Russia rules one continuous empire, despotically. Can we counter her with a loose alliance of economic rivals, each serving its own exclusive interests? For an equivalent strength must we not move toward Mr. Pearson's Atlantic Community?

Such arguments, however, are still based on fear. And will fear endow us with the character to change our bad habits drastically? Is not the source of character the moral law within us? A generous disinterested deed is demanded if we are to reach our true greatness. Let us do it without hatred of yesterday's "gallant" friends or tomorrow's. Let us do it from a sense of duty; for this was always the destiny of the West.

Clearly it is also our duty to be strong, lest materialism and a slavery to earthly things be forced upon us. How better can we grow strong than in friendship and trust with the sharers of our faith? And since that faith teaches the sanctity of every man, why should the world fear us if we serve it? But if we seek strength solely for a cold or a hot war, in a mood of high selfishness, why should the world have confidence?

In practical terms, if we are to escape from fear, from perilously big government, from Moloch-nationalism, we must restore the relatively free movement of money and goods and men. We must begin with our own corners of the earth where Westerners and their descendents live. And we cannot do it while preserving the monstrous fiction that each nation's "interests" are absolute — especially since one nation is strong enough to swamp all the others if we insist on beggar-my-neighbor.

We shall be no use to starving millions elsewhere if we impoverish ourselves, waging economic civil war behind a façade of "defense." We strengthen each other with arms, grants, and pacts, while weakening each other with tariffs, quotas, currency controls, prohibitions on immigration, and every convenient device for making our total Western economy inefficient. Our brothers in faith and tradition are called "them": we all suspect each other of sharp practice.

We can begin building our society at any moment, by admitting that economic and foreign policy must be pooled if "defense" is to be more than an incantation. We may even be on the verge of this brave move. But partnership, abiding and trustworthy, demands higher imagination. Great evils are not cured by little devices. Nothing can gain us the world's confidence until we the Western peoples give permission to our rulers to start exorcising the demon of absolute sovereignty. Then only would our shared strength suffice to relieve us from fear. Then only would it give us the privilege of helping our less lucky neighbors.

Here is a cure for the frustrations of modern man. We know the times are out of joint but we feel helpless before the magnitude of our troubles. Yet we alone, the people alone, can shoulder this responsibility. It is for us, not for our rulers, to join together and give the liberating word. This is the true democracy. We have seen that majority rule can be poisonous if uncontrolled by conscience, for man's power of evil passes understanding. But so does his power of good. When a decision touching the whole of life is to be made, rejuvenating the moral base of a society, no one can issue the orders except Everyman.

Here is the noblest cause in centuries. The West, by an act of will, can save itself and send hope to humanity. No other people today could extend such hope — although the communists would be glad to try. "Le devoir ne cesse que là où le pouvoir manque." We have the power and therefore the duty. How shall we be forgiven if we lack the will? How escape the gloomy future predicted by T. S. Eliot:

In the land of lobelias and tennis flannels
The rabbit shall burrow and the thorn revisit,
The nettle shall flourish on the gravel court,
And the wind shall say, "Here were decent godless people:
Their only monument the asphalt road
And a thousand lost golf balls."

Conclusion

✿　　✿　　✿　　✿　　✿

Conclusion

✱　　✱　　✱　　✱　　✱

We have tried to explore some aspects of our heritage, "to recover these ideas, to 'call them in,' as gold and silver coins used to be called in for reminting." And we have tried to use terms which may be taken spiritually by the Christian, substantially by the non-Christian. We believe this is neither dishonest nor misleading so long as we confess what we are doing, for each article of our faith may fairly be put in religious or in worldly language.

Freedom of conscience or constitutional government; the natural law of Thomas Aquinas, or "reason" in the English common law; the natural piety of Virgil and Bernanos, or "conservation" preached by such writers as Michael Roberts and Fairfield Osborn; the absolute truth of Sophocles, or the truth which Oliver Wendell Holmes "cannot help believing": these pairs of phrases, we admit, are not merely two ways of saying the same thing. The things themselves are different in their Christian and in their secular forms. Yet happily they have much in common. The spiritual does not contradict the material meaning: it accepts the material and goes farther.

No man can hope to possess more than a small part of our heritage. But even a small part may give a clue to the pattern of the whole. Have we uncovered such a clue, which might help us to recapture our lost unity? What would the world feel like if these traditions, which we have sought to describe, were in fact our common traditions and if upon them we built a common life?

No faith could transform us into angels, so the West would doubtless remain partly quarrelsome, partly jealous. Yet if the West were indeed to be revived — proud of its past, aware of its meaning in history and of its brotherhood — we should easily transcend the broken and embittered community of today.

In the first place we should no longer resemble the Greek city-states in the fury of our self-destruction. The Greeks treated the members of a neighboring city as "things," not as personalities — and so it was permissible to compel a war, to kill all the men and sell all the women like so much meat. The West, to be sure, has committed equivalent crimes, but only when she was failing in her duty. The Greeks were not failing according to their own lights; neither were the Romans when they extinguished the liberties of their world; they were merely "patriotic." The natural law was still a dream of philosophers, not yet a fact of life.

No one who believes in that law and in the freedom of the

spirit can be without pity for man's predicament, or without a sense of sharing in the general guilt. No society founded upon those beliefs can be rank with the self-esteem of modern nationalism — can be confident that "*our* conscience is clear," that while the world decays the fault lies wholly with other men. The West, if true to itself, will never choose to unite in a league of righteousness pledged to put down the sins of others. But it may unite in a league of humility, to help itself to be less sinful, less avaricious at the expense of its fellow citizens, and thus stronger and abler to help all men. The strength would come not from fear — but as all good things do come, from trying to obey the law of nature. Grace bestows faith; humility bestows strength; man saves his life by being willing to lose it.

Similarly, if we build this larger area of collaboration, which is the true West, we may fulfill man's hopes for less war — because we shall be seeking the good rather than giving way to fear of evil. Fear leads to alliances, which may win wars but which seldom prevent them. Faith leads to friendship, to a knowledge that we are dealing always with human personalities, never with abstractions: always with men and women, never with "communists." And this in turn leads to generosity, to a sense of the larger tragedy which embraces our enemies as well as ourselves and which might help us (if we are given time) to reverse the verdict of the nineteenth century and begin again to entice Russia westward.

This tenderness for humanity even in our enemies, this ability to share the blame for our common tragedy and thus to feel a Christian love for the very people we are fighting, belongs to what we call chivalry. It is what Lincoln had in mind — during the civil war which he accepted and which he intended to win — when he repeated that all the law and the prophets are in our Lord's commandments concerning love.

In 1625, during the Thirty Years' War, the Dutch garrison at Breda surrendered to a Spanish Army under a Genoese leader, the Marquis of Spinola. One of the greatest of Velasquez's pictures recalls the scene. Justin of Nassau bows submissively as he offers the keys of the town; but Spinola refuses, laying his hand gently, chivalrously, on the shoulder of his beaten foe. The General had given orders that officers and men were to march out of the town "with flying colors, drums beating, completely armed. . . . No soldier shall be questioned or detained for any cause or pretext whatsoever. . . . And it shall be lawful for them to take with them their wives, children, household staffs, horses and carts."

Throughout the previous century Spanish armies had been infamous for their malice. Yet here was an act of charity and faith which has become proverbial, which will never be forgotten. We respond to such beauty of conduct as naturally as we respond to a blow in the face: kindness is as contagious as rage.

When General Grant met General Lee at Appomattox Court House to receive the surrender of the Army of Northern Virginia he offered a peace of honor. Three days later he assigned General Chamberlain to receive formally the arms and colors of Lee's regiments. Magnificently, Chamberlain ordered for the defeated foe a salute of arms. He wrote,

> I sought no authority, nor asked forgiveness. Before us in proud humiliation stood the embodiment of manhood: men whom neither toils nor sufferings, nor the fact of death, nor disaster, nor hopelessness could bend from their resolve; standing before us now, thin, worn, and famished, but erect, and with eyes looking level into ours. . . . Our bugle sounds the signal and instantly our whole line from right to left, regiment by regiment in succession, gives the soldier's salutation, from the "order arms" to the old "carry" — the marching salute. . . . Not a sound of trumpet more, nor roll of drum; not a cheer, nor word nor whisper of vainglorying . . . but an awed stillness rather, and breath-holding, as if it were the passing of the dead. . . . How could we help falling on our knees, all of us together, and praying God to pity and forgive us all!

These are not old tales from an impossible past. Spinola and General Chamberlain are children of the West, and if "all generations are equidistant from eternity" we have a right to claim that they stand beside us today, teaching us to see in our enemies "the embodiment of manhood," counseling us to pray for pity and forgiveness on both sides. But in whose name do Westerners pray, if not that of the Christian God? And if many of us find Him unacceptable, have we a basis for unity?

The questions are clearly unanswerable. But we can say

in hopefulness (because grace does truly bestow faith) that if we define our West, and feel it, and serve it, and seek to unite it, the very act of service and dedication may some day bring us home.

And let us remember that all the children of the classical past and Christian Middle Ages are included in "the West." When we speak in the name of our great heritage we do not speak solely of the Protestant and agnostic North or of the Catholic and anticlerical South, of the New World or of the Old, of socialist planning or of private enterprise.

The West has seen the rise and fall of many political systems — and of many aberrations, such as modern fascism or the seventeenth-century "state." Always the aberrations have denied our common faith in freedom. Always we have defeated them, and have then sought to bring their authors back into our camp. Let us not impair the record by seeking an unhistorical exclusiveness today.

Western countries with similar political habits and a common literature, such as Great Britain and the United States, may discover a special closeness in their relations; and all those whose governments are "democratic" may find a special bond. Thus the nations of the North Atlantic will doubtless be the first to join in a political union, if the West is ever to reassemble her scattered members. But let us not form a union of moral superiority — or how shall we make converts and spread outwards? How shall we re-educate ourselves into humility and strength if we look askance at neighbors who share our ultimate faith but whom we consider insufficiently democratic or freedom-loving?

Who but God can decide whether the workman in a Detroit factory loves freedom more than the Spanish farmer, the Italian stonemason, the Argentine cowboy? There are many roads to liberty, including the anarchic distaste for government which makes the Mediterranean peoples a curse to bureaucrats. There are many roads to servitude, including the self-idolatrous folly of those who praise the present attack on the civil rights of Americans, in the name of "Americanism."

John Milton tells us that Truth "came once into the world with her divine Master, and was a perfect shape most glorious to look on." But later, when He ascended, her virgin form was hewed into a thousand pieces and scattered to the winds. "From that time ever since, the sad friends of Truth, such as durst appear, imitating the careful search that Isis made for the mangled body of Osiris, went up and down gathering up limb by limb still as they could find them. We have not yet found them all, Lords and Commons, nor ever shall do, till her Master's second coming."

Remembering this admonition we can seek to possess our heritage, and to take pride therein, without arrogating all virtue to one small part of our society. If we can thus re-learn respect and sympathy and fellow-feeling for those who live within the Wall of the Classical-Christian world, we shall discover that almost without effort we extend the same feelings to mankind. Our Wall will be not an exclusion but an invitation to enter.

And we may hope that many will enter, beginning with the Russians. But first we must show that within the Wall we are trying to live as fellow citizens, not to promote snarling small "pools of self-esteem"; that we are trying to blame "the troubles of our proud and angry dust" upon ourselves, not upon foreign demons; that we are trying to protect the precious area of freedom which long ago we wrested from the lords of this world.

Notes

✿   ✿   ✿   ✿   ✿

Notes

*   *   *

Page

3. "As to your entreaty . . . " Sir Frederick Whyte, *China and Foreign Powers*, 2d and rev. ed. (Oxford University Press, 1928), p. 41.

6. "The generations of the past . . . " H. Butterfield, *Christianity and History* (J. Bell & Sons, London, 1949), pp. 65–66. As Professor Butterfield makes clear, the famous statement about "Every generation . . . " is taken from Ranke.

7. "Slogans are apt . . . " *The Saturday Review of Literature*, Vol. XXXIV, No. 15, p. 14.

13. "Why . . . must we fly . . . " C. G. Le Boutillier, *American Democracy and Natural Law* (Columbia University Press, 1950), p. 100.

"a sufficiently earthbound body . . . " Sir Frederick Pollock, *Essays in Law* (Macmillan, London, 1922), pp. 57, 69.

30. "In the lurid light . . . " *A Study of History* (Oxford University Press, 1934), Vol. V, pp. 670–71.

31. "a despair hard to realize . . ." *Rome* (Henry Holt, New York, 1912), p. 187.

40. "and then made a tour . . ." *Dictionary of National Biography* (Oxford University Press, 1937–38), Vol. X, p. 710.

41. "Thus, at one stroke . . ." *A Study of History* (Oxford University Press, 1939), Vol. IV, p. 151, note 2.

43. "The bitter conflict . . ." Milton Waldman, *The Lady Mary*, MS iv, 32–33.

48. "The communism of the East . . ." Leslie Paul, *The Age of Terror* (Faber & Faber, London, 1950), p. 148.

50. "Man is a beast of prey . . ." Oswald Spengler, *The Hour of Decision* (Allen & Unwin, London, 1934), p. 21.

52. "For he that performeth . . ." *Leviathan*, Part I, Chapter XIV, pp. 124–25 (ed. of 1839).

78. "A certain massive fairness . . ." M. P. Charlesworth, *The Roman Empire* (Oxford University Press, 1951), p. 25.

84. "gave order and system . . ." M. Rostovtzeff, *A History of the Ancient World* (Oxford University Press, 1926), Vol. II, pp. 327, 331.

88. "L'Europe angoissée . . ." Maurice Duverger, *Le Monde*, 14 July 1951.

   "Les frontières de la Russie . . ." François Mauriac, *Figaro*, 16 Jan. 1951.

89. "The oblivious Caesars . . ." Evelyn Waugh, *Helena* (Chapman & Hall, London, 1950), p. 139.

94. "What the slave was . . ." Lord Acton, "The History of Freedom in Antiquity," in *Essays on Freedom and Power* (The Beacon Press, Boston, 1948).

103. "Grèce fort peu romanisée . . ." Wladimir Weidlé, *La Russie Absente et Présente* (Gallimard, Paris, 1949), pp. 15–16, 26.

136. "For the *divine* will . . ." Emmanuel Kant, *The Moral Law.*

142. "The three generations of the Socratic school . . ." Lord Acton, *The Quarterly Review*, January 1878. Reprinted in *The History of Freedom and Other Essays* (Macmillan, London, 1907).

146. "mile upon mile, from snow to desert . . ." Evelyn Waugh, *Helena* (Chapman & Hall, London, 1950), p. 47.

150. "Let every man abide . . ." I Cor., VII, 20–24.

153. "the law of nature was . . . a familiar idea . . ." Richard O'Sullivan, K.C., *Natural Law and Common Law* (The Crotius Society, London, 1946).

160. "The solid scholar . . ." *Western Political Thought* (Jonathan Cape, London, 1947), p. 302.

161. "He is born capable . . ." Georges Bernanos, *Les grands cimetières sous la lune* (Librairie Plon, Paris, 1938).

173. "The nation, which the age of Enlightenment . . ." Carl Becker, *The Declaration of Independence* (Alfred A. Knopf, New York, 1942), p. 290.

175. "at once a rest from responsibility . . ." Michael Roberts, *The Estate of Man* (Faber & Faber, London, 1951), pp. 115–16.

178. "Industrialism . . . is the systematic exploitation . . ." *Themes and Variations* (Chatto & Windus, London, 1950), pp. 228, 230, 234.

"modern civilization is based . . ." *The Estate of Man* (Faber & Faber, London, 1951), pp. 33, 56, 57.

191. "It is possible that the strain . . ." Henry Clay, in *The State of Society* (Oxford Press, 1940), pp. 130–31.

192. "There is little doubt . . ." Michael Roberts, *The Estate of Man* (Faber & Faber, London, 1951), p. 91.

196. " 'The People' has become 'The nation' . . ." *The Historical Evolution of Modern Nationalism* (Macmillan, New York, 1931), p. 69.

202. "What is left for modern man . . ." *The Belief in Progress* (Oxford University Press, 1950), p. 180.

205. "a religious conviction . . ." *The Recovery of the West* (Faber & Faber, London, 1941), pp. 314–15. (Roberts tells us that the book was planned, and for the most part written, before the outbreak of the war.)

207. "It provides . . . against the servility . . ." "Nationality," in *The Home and Foreign Review*, July 1862.

209. "Poor men that we are . . ." *Englishmen, Frenchmen, Spaniards* (Oxford University Press, 1928), p. 243.

217. "to recover these ideas . . ." George Bernanos, *Tradition of Freedom* (Dennis Dobson, London, 1950), p. 27.

223. "came once in the world with her divine Master . . ." *Areopagitica.*

Index

*   *   *   *   *

Index

*   *   *